UMBR(A)

IGNORANCE OF THE LAW

UMBR(a)

A JOURNAL OF THE UNCONSCIOUS   2003

ISSN 1087-0830   ISBN 0-9666452-6-X

EDITOR:
Alissa Lea Jones

EDITORIAL COMMITTEE:
Mike Baxter
Trisha Brady
Eugenie Brinkema
Sorin Cucu
Erica DeSanto
Alexei Di Orio
Theresa Giron
Li-chun Hsiao
Alissa Lea Jones
Sooyoung Kang
Sean Kelly
Cristina Laurita
Alan Lopez
Anthony Siu
Andrew Skomra
Barbara Straumann
Mikko Tuhkanen
Roland Végső

COVER DESIGN:
Sam Gillespie

IMAGES EDITORS:
Theresa Giron
Alissa Lea Jones
Andrew Skomra

UMBR(a) is published with the help of grants from the following organizations and individuals at the State University of New York at Buffalo:

The Graduate Student Association*
The Center for the Study of Psychoanalysis and Culture
The Group for the Discussion of the Freudian Field
The English Department
The English Graduate Student Association
The James H. McNulty Chair (Dennis Tedlock)

*The views expressed herein do not necessarily reflect those of the GSA.

Address for Editorial and Subscription Enquiries:

UMBR(a)
Center for the Study of Psychoanalysis and Culture
SUNY/Buffalo, North Campus
409 Clemens Hall
Buffalo, NY 14260-4610
http://wings.buffalo.edu/student-life/graduate/gsa/lacan/lacan.html

DISTRIBUTION:
Erica DeSanto

FACULTY ADVISOR:
Joan Copjec

CONTENTS

4   EDITORIAL: IGNORANCE OF THE LAW...
     alissa lea jones

9   THE SUBJECT
     étienne balibar

25   OMNITUDO REALITATIS
     marina de carneri

39   LACK AND DESTRUCTION
     alain badiou

63   LACK OF BEING, DENIAL OF GOOD
     candace vogler

81   LACAN AT THE LIMITS OF LEGAL THEORY:
     LAW, DESIRE, AND SOVEREIGN VIOLENCE
     steven miller

97   BEING HUMAN: BESTIALITY, ANTHROPOPHAGY, AND LAW
     kalpana seshadri-crooks

117 THE LURE OF ANTIGONE:
     APORIAS OF AN ETHICS OF THE POLITICAL
     yannis stavrakakis

131 "WHAT SOME WOULD CALL...":
     A RESPONSE TO YANNIS STAVRAKAKIS
     slavoj žižek

136 REVIEWS

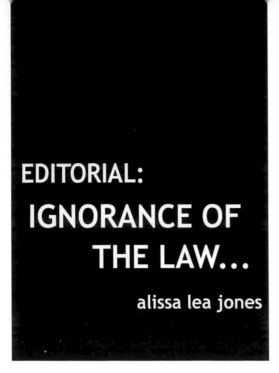

EDITORIAL:
IGNORANCE OF THE LAW...

alissa lea jones

Just as psychoanalysis is full of well-wrought, if sometimes only half-understood, maxims, so too the law clings to certain axiomatic pronouncements, the meanings of which often become lost in the frequency with which they are deployed. One such precept — at once a foundational legal principle and perhaps the most overworked cliché the law has to offer — provides the basis for our title: "Ignorance of the law is no excuse." An elementary principle of the criminal law, it holds that no individual may avail himself, for the purposes of a legal defense, of an ignorance of the law. The law presumes, in other words, that all citizens know the law.

The psychoanalytic ear is no doubt pricked. It notes first the ambiguity of the sentence construction, an ambiguity that apparently goes unrecognized by legal administrators. Ignorance here only ever refers to the ignorance of the legal subject. Psychoanalysis has no quarrel with the proposition of an ignorant subject — arguably psychoanalysis *invented* this subject. What psychoanalysis would object to, however, is the law's attribution of ignorance to the subject alone. Although the law rather unproblematically situates (even as it refuses to acknowledge) ignorance on the side of its subject, it is in fact an absent subject to whom an ignorance is imputed. As such, the sentence allows for an alternative reading: there may be an ignorance operative in the law itself.

If what is at issue is ignorance, we ought to ask where it is that knowledge resides. Lacan is quite clear on this point: the locus of knowledge is the Other — the Law. This would appear to square with the customary understanding of the "Ignorance of the law…" dictum, which assumes not that the criminal study up on whatever particular law he would then violate, but rather that all citizens have at least a minimum of legal literacy based on an implicit appeal to a generalized set of (moral) principles supposed to govern human behavior. The wager is that even those who are not especially well-versed in legal particularities will somehow intuit the illegality of their criminal misdeeds. The implication here is that the law functions as its own warrant, that there is a guarantee that any particular law is knowable and, furthermore, is legitimate by virtue of the omniscience and ultimate authority of the big Other. Psychoanalysis, however, suggests otherwise. The Other may be the place of knowledge (or, more properly, the place where knowledge is placed), but, as Lacan points out, "[t]he hitch is that the Other, the locus, knows nothing."[1] In psychoanalysis, there is no guarantee.

The question is, then: How does the law continue to function — and function effectively — when the law is itself ignorant? Not surprisingly, psychoanalysis locates the successful operation of the law precisely in its paradoxical status. Freud's myth of the primal horde, with the killing of the primal father, remains the most compelling elaboration of this paradox. The murder of the father — the father as the perceived obstacle to the fulfillment of the sons' desire — does not pave the way for the enjoyment the sons seek but rather strengthens the prohibition against it. In Freud's genealogy, there is no clear distinction between the brothers' law and the father's autocratic rule, the contract only ever being the legally enforced repression of that which brought it into existence in the first place. It is thus what Lacan refers to as a "passion for ignorance"[2] — a desire not to know — that is the very condition of the proper functioning of the law. Law's subject wants to know nothing of its desire, and it is this desire, this passion for ignorance, that sustains the law even in its ignorance. What psychoanalysis claims with respect to ignorance and the law is thus a substantial revision of the legal principle: it is not that ignorance of the law is *no* excuse (for violating it); it is rather that ignorance of the law is the *only* excuse (for following it).

Such a revision suggests a wholly different relation between the subject and the law. Implicit in the legal rejection of ignorance as an excuse for transgression is the law's own "theory of the subject" (to borrow the title of Alain Badiou's 1982 monograph, an excerpt of which appears in translation in the pages that follow): the law equates the subject with knowledge of the law. That is to say, the legal citizen/subject only rightfully assumes such a position when it is no longer ignorant of the law. The law, however, does not simply produce the effect that it names (the subject that knows the law), but always something more than that, an excess, a desire that it cannot but fail to contain. And it is there in this failure of the law that psychoanalysis locates its subject. For psychoanalysis, it is only by way of the law's ignorance that the subject comes into being. It is this incompleteness or lack that allows for the possibility of a desiring subject, a subject that is not simply a determinate effect of the law.

To acknowledge the generative quality of the lack in the Other is not to suggest that the law isn't forever attempting to conceal it. Perhaps the most spectacular recent example of this is the now-familiar image — the one that graces our cover — of U.S. Attorney General John Ashcroft standing in front of the bare-breasted statue which has for some seventy years symbolized justice for the department bearing that name. The fury that erupted in response to Ashcroft's decision to conceal the Spirit of Justice's offending breast was not over the inordinate expenditure of money he authorized for a set of drapes ($8,000 is nothing in terms of typical government spending). It was not that veiling the statue offended our aesthetic sensibilities (it's not, after all, a particularly remarkable piece of sculpture). It is rather that we were confronted with the ignorance of the law and, more significantly, the extraordinary lengths to which the law will go to disguise that fact. In the case of Ashcroft and Minnie Lou (as she's known around the DOJ), the law (or Ashcroft as its guardian) was standing right there in front of the spirit or desire that ostensibly animates it, and Ashcroft *covers her up*. (That he executed the veiling of the statue in the wake of the September 11 terrorist attacks when he was initiating all manner of injustice against both the so-called enemy and his own people cannot be mere coincidence.)

What Ashcroft's fetishistic logic makes painfully clear is that the legal enterprise is not necessarily an ethical one, and it is precisely this sort of logic that psychoanalysis aims to subvert. Psychoanalysis is neither a theoretical apparatus nor a clinical methodology; it is an ethical practice. Psychoanalytic practice turns the ignorance of desire upon which the law rests into knowledge. It produces a subject that acts on the basis of its desire, and this is a subject considered dangerous in the eyes of the law. For this is someone the law cannot control, someone for whom nothing — certainly not a set of chintzy drapes — can stand as obstacle to his desire. The psychoanalytic subject assumes as its own the desire that the law can never truly conceal. Now, does this mean that we believe justice is possible? No, but this doesn't stop us from trying to create it. And that is what Lacan called the ethics of psychoanalysis.

All of this is to say that, ultimately, the problem with the legal formulation rests not in the indeterminacy of its subject, but in the opposition it constructs between ignorance and knowledge. Psychoanalysis, of course, accepts no such dichotomy. For psychoanalysis posits a different kind of knowledge, a "knowledge that is not known."[3] Such knowledge may properly be described as ignorance, an ignorance that is not simply a lack of information, but an active refusal of it: an ignorance that knows. And it is on the basis of such ignorance, "on the basis of a kind of refusal of understanding that we push open the door to analytic understanding."[4] We proceed, then, as does any properly psychoanalytic inquiry: in ignorance. The essays collected here examine the various ways in which these mutually constitutive terms — the law, the subject, ignorance — might be knotted. Such a collection assumes that while ignorance of the law — the ignorance that is the law and our ignorance as subjects of it — may be inevitable, ignorance of this fact is, indeed, inexcusable.

1. Jacques Lacan, *The Seminar of Jacques Lacan, Book XX: Encore: On Feminine Sexuality, The Limits of Love and Knowledge, 1972-1973*, ed. Jacques-Alain Miller, trans. Bruce Fink (New York: Norton, 1998), 98.

2. Ibid., 121.

3. Ibid., 96.

4. Lacan, *The Seminar of Jacques Lacan, Book I: Freud's Papers on Technique, 1953-1954*, ed. Jacques-Alain Miller, trans. John Forrester (New York: Norton, 1988), 73.

RZECZPOSPOLITA POLSKA   REPUBLIQUE POLONAISE

No. 02285

PASZPORT-PASSEPORT

Obywatelka(a) Polski(a)   Wojciechowski Miroslaw
Citoyen(ne) polonais(e)

Zamieszkały w   Torunia
Domicilié à

Rysopis
Signalements

Rok urodzenia   1917
Date de naissance

Miejsce urodzenia   Zoppot
Lieu de naissance

Stan   Kawaler
Etat civil

Zatrudnienie   Kupiec
Profession

Taille

Twarz   podłużna
Visage

Włosy   jasne
Cheveux

Oczy   jasne
Yeux

Znaki szczególne
Signes particuliers

Kraje, na które niniejszy paszport jest ważny wszystkich krajów w Europie i poza Europą
Pays pour lesquels ce passeport est valable   tous les pays d'Europe et hors d'Europe

Uprasza się wszystkie Władze Państw Cudzoziemskich oraz poleca się
Les Autorités des Etats Etrangers sont priées et les Autorités polonaises

wszystkim Władzom Polskim okazać w razie potrzeby pomoc i opiekę
osobom wymienionym w paszporcie.
sont requises de prêter au porteur aide et assistance en cas de nécessité.

Termin ważności paszportu upływa dniem
Ce passeport expire le trzydziestego września 1940

o ile nie będzie wznowiony.
à moins de renouvellement.

Bukareszt 1939

TADEUSZ STAPIŃSKI
Wicekonsul R. P.

THE SUBJECT
étienne balibar

NIETZSCHE AND THE IMPOSSIBILITY OF TRANSLATION

The category of the subject is more central to philosophy now than ever before, especially for those trends reformulated in the twentieth century. At the heart of the problem is a more or less explicit "play of words" found in the Latin etymology of the term: on the one hand, we have the neutral term *subjectum* that philosophers since scholasticism have considered as the translation of the Greek *hupokeimenon* (substratum or support); on the other hand, we have the masculine term *subjectus*, which is understood to be equivalent to the medieval *subditus* (subordinate). The former gave rise to a line of logico-grammatical and ontologico-transcendental meanings; the latter to a juristic, political, and theological semantic tradition. Far from remaining distinct, since Kant, the two traditions have overdetermined one another around the problematics of "subjectivity" and "subjectivation." This relationship of mutual determination, however, is alternately emphasized or repressed depending on whether or not it is in the philosopher's interest to bring the concept of the subject up to date by *working* on it.

As an introduction to these problems in modern philosophy, we will reread an amazing passage from Nietzsche's *Beyond Good and Evil*:

> Philosophers tend to talk about the will as if it were the most familiar thing in the world...A person who *wills* —, commands something inside himself that obeys, or that he believes to obey [*commande en lui-même à quelque chose qui obéit ou dont il se croit obéi; befiehlt einem Etwas in sich, das gehorcht oder von dem er glaubt, dass es gehorcht*]. But now we notice the strangest thing about the will — about this multifarious thing that people have only one word for. On the one hand, we are, under the circumstances, both the one who commands *and* the one who obeys [*à la fois celui qui commande et celui qui obéit; zugleich die Befehlenden und Gehorchenden*], and as the obedient one [*en tant que sujet obéissant; als Gehorchende*] we are familiar with the feelings of compulsion, force, pressure, resistance, and motion that generally start right after the act of willing. On the other hand, however, we are in the habit of ignoring and deceiving ourselves about this

duality by means of the synthetic concept of the "I" [*nous duper nous-mêmes en escamotant cette dualité grâce au concept synthétique du "moi"; uns über diese Zweiheit vermöge des synthetischen Begriffs "ich" hinwegzusetzen, hinwegzutäuschen*]..."Freedom of the will" — that is the word for the multi-faceted state of pleasure of one who commands and, at the same time, identifies himself with the accomplished act of willing [*le mot qui désigne ce complexe état d'euphorie du sujet voulant, qui commande et s'identifie à la fois avec l'exécuteur de l'action; das Wort für jenen vielfachen Lust-Zustand des Wollenden, der befiehlt und sich zugleich mit dem Ausführenden als Eins setzt*]...Accordingly, the one who wills takes his feeling of pleasure as the commander, and adds to it the feelings of pleasure from the successful instruments that carry out the task [*le sujet voulant ajoute ainsi les sentiments de plaisir issus des instruments d'exécution; Der Wollende nimmt dergestalt die Lustgefühle der ausführenden, erfolgreichen Werkzeuge*], as well as from the useful "under-wills" or under-souls [*"sous-volontés" ou sous-âmes; "Unterwillen" oder Unterseelen*] — our body is, after all, only a society constructed out of many souls [*un édifice d'âmes multiples; ein Gesellschaftsbau vieler Seelen*]. *L'effet c'est moi* [in French in the original text]: what happens here is what happens in every well-constructed and happy community: the ruling class identifies itself with the successes of the community [*la classe dirigeante s'identifie au succès de la collectivité; dass die regierende Klasse sich mit den Erfolgen des Gemeinwesens identifizieren*].[1]

My point is not to challenge the French translation but to call attention to the problems it reveals. We have to attribute a particular significance to the fact that Nietzsche's text itself contains a reflection on translation as a process of deception that is endowed with a fundamental anthropological significance. Considering the inherent illusions of the unity of the will, it is not unexpected that the invocation of the political metaphor (if such a thing exists) is accompanied by a *French* phrase (thus something "untranslatable") that parodies Louis XIV's "*L'État, c'est moi*," the famous allegory of absolute monarchy.

By systematically introducing the word "*sujet*" (*sujet obéissant, sujet voulant*), the translation posits an *etwas* that would be identical in both the act of commanding and the effect of obeying, and thereby also circumvents the critique that Nietzsche's text directs at the illusion of the "I." On the other hand, in playing with the connotations of the French word "*sujet*" not conveyed by the strict German equivalent "*das Subjekt*," the translation uses a generic term to express the ambivalences of the real or imaginary relations of subordination (*arkhein* and *arkhesthai*) between the "parts of the soul" that, for Nietzsche, constitute the essence of the "will": the "obedient subject" appears to be a tautology and the "willing subject," a quasi-contradiction. Or is it the other way around?

This text throws us right in the middle of the linguistic tensions that characterize the construction and use of the concept of the "subject." These tensions are defined by the tendency toward two separate paradigms of interpretation of the subject: one peculiar to neo-Latin languages (especially French), the other peculiar to German. In the first case, the simultaneously logico-ontological and juridico-political connotation of the subject (sustained by a certain "historical play of words" between the meanings of *subjectum* and *subjectus*) is exploited in a systematic investigation of the modalities of the "subjectivation of the subject." In the other case — where the political dimension is obscured by language, or rather, is relegated to the latent system of translations — the relation between the mode of existence of the subject and the register of law or power is located exclusively on the side of an ontology of freedom that opposes it to nature. These two paradigms, of course, are not developed independently of each other: they share all their classical references, and the more or less simultaneous translation of the works of European metaphysics is one of the main sources of their history. In this respect, it is apparent how revealing the divergent readings of Nietzsche's work prove to be here.

THE "CARTESIAN" SUBJECT: A KANTIAN INVENTION

The expressions "Cartesian subject" and "Cartesian subjectivity" are so common and so often function to situate Cartesian thought in historical or comparative schemes that it is worth the trouble to expose the conditions of its invention, which is also a *quid pro quo* of translation. This *quid pro quo*, however, is a testimony to an extraordinary conceptual work in the midst of language itself (which started with the syntactical charts of Latin, French, and German). It is sufficiently powerful and suggestive to induce a retroactive understanding of Descartes' text and the stakes of his philosophy from which we cannot extract ourselves. Coming after Kant's reading of Descartes, we can at most read in the latter an anticipated resistance to the transcendental problematic, but cannot rescue him from the language of subjectivity. In this sense, the effects of Kant's intervention are irreversible.

Subjektivität — that is, the field and quality of the phenomena within the thinking, perceiving, and sentient individual that are not the effects of exterior objects affecting it but of its own dispositions (what Locke and Malebranche called "secondary qualities") — is already an important term in Baumgarten's *Aesthetics*. Joachim Ritter is right in reminding us of this fact, although his use of *subjectum* — or rather of the German "*Subjekt*" — is subsequent and not prior to this abstract conceptual formation. In reality, it is only after the *Critique of Pure Reason* that the *Subjekt* becomes the key concept of a philosophy of subjectivity (according to its different qualifications: the logical subject, the empirical subject, the rational subject, the transcendental subject, the moral subject). On the one hand, Kant's philosophy *invents* the problematic of a thought for which its access to the objectivity of the laws of nature, as well as to the universality of ethical and aesthetic values, reside in its own constitution. On the other hand, that philosophy *names* as the "subject" (that is to say, the other of the object) the general individuality immanent to the play of the faculties of consciousness which, for all finite souls, constitutes the world and confers meaning on action within it. Even if one takes into consideration the rather extraordinary anticipations of the concept (like that identified by Alain de Libera in the thirteenth-century Franciscan "spiritualist" Pierre-Jean Olieu) — of which it remains to be seen how they could have been known by Kant — the only intrinsic link between this Kantian creation of the *Subjekt* and the scholastic notion of *subjectum* or *suppositum* is precisely the one indicated by the idea of the Copernican revolution: after this revolution the categories of predication are no longer of the order of being, but rather are rules internal to thinking. They are not categories of being but categories of the subject, constitutive of the object (and in this sense of experience in general, transcendentals).

Why was it necessary for Kant to project this discovery retrospectively onto Descartes, giving credence to the idea of the Cartesian invention of the subject and inciting even the greatest to search for the traces of a semantic mutation of terms practically never used by Descartes himself? The answer resides in Kant's text. Let me juxtapose three passages from the *Critique of Pure Reason* that are, one has to confess, not always easy to translate:

1) Das: *Ich denke*, muss alle meine Vorstellungen begleiten können; denn sonst würde etwas in mir vorgestellt werden, was garnicht gedacht werden könnte...Also hat alles Mannigfaltige der Anschauung eine notwendige Beziehung auf das: *Ich denke*, in demselben Subjekt, darin dieses Mannigfaltige angetroffen wird. Diese Vorstellung aber ist ein Aktus der Spontaneität, sie kann nicht als zur Sinnlichkeit gehörig angesehen werden. Ich nenne sie die reine Apperzeption...weil sie dasjenige Selbstbewusstsein ist, was, indem es die Vorstellung *Ich denke* hervorbringt, die alle anderen muss begleiten können, und in allem Bewusstsein ein und dasselbe ist...von keiner weiter begleitet werden kann.

The *I think* must be *capable* of accompanying all my presentations. For otherwise something would be presented to me that could not be thought at all....Hence everything manifold in intuition has a necessary reference to the *I think* in the same subject in whom this manifold is found. But this presentation [i.e., the *I think*] is an act of spontaneity; i.e., it cannot be regarded as belonging to sensibility. I call it *pure apperception*....for it is the self-consciousness which, because it produces the presentation *I think* that must be capable of accompanying all other presentations[,] and [because it] is one and the same in all consciousness, cannot be accompanied by any further presentation.[2]

2) *Ich*, als denkend, bin ein Gegenstand des inneren Sinnes, und heisse Seele....Demnach bedeutet der Ausdruck: Ich, als ein denkend Wesen, schon den Gegenstand der Psychologie....Ich denke, ist also der alleinige Text der rationalen Psychologie, aus welchem sie ihre ganze Weisheit auswickeln soll. Man sieht leicht, dass dieser Gedanke, wenn er auf einen Gegenstand (mich selbst) bezogen werden soll, nichts anderes, als transzendentale Prädikate desselben, enthalten könne....Zum Grunde derselben können wir aber nichts anderes legen, als die einfache und für sich selbst an Inhalt gänzlich leere Vorstellung: *Ich*; von der man nicht einmal sagen kann, dass sie ein Begriff sei, sondern ein blosses Bewusstsein, das alle Begriffe begleitet. Durch dieses Ich, oder Er, oder Es

(das Ding), welches denkt, wird nun nichts weiter, als ein transzendentales Subjekt der Gedanken vorgestellt = x, welches nur durch die Gedanken, die seine Prädikate sind, erkannt wird.

I, as thinking, am an object of inner sense and am called soul....Thus the expression, I, as a thinking being, already means the object of psychology....Hence *I think* is rational psychology's sole text, from which it is to unfold its entire wisdom. We readily see that if this thought is to be referred to an object (myself), then it can contain nothing but transcendental predicates of this object....Yet we can lay at the basis of this science [rational psychology] nothing but the simple, and by itself quite empty, presentation *I*, of which we cannot even say that it is a concept, but only that it is a mere consciousness accompanying all concepts. Now through this *I* or *he* or *it* (the thing) that thinks, nothing more is presented than a transcendental subject of thoughts = x. This subject is cognized only through the thoughts that are its predicates. (383-385)

3) Der Satz: *Ich denke*, wird aber hierbei nur problematisch genommen; nicht sofern er eine Wahrnehmung von einem Dasein enthalten mag, (das Cartesianische *cogito, ergo sum*,) sondern seiner blossen Möglichkeit nach, um zu sehen, welche Eigenschaften aus diesem so einfachen Satze auf das Subjekt desselben (es mag dergleichen nun existieren oder nicht) fliessen mögen. Läge unserer reinen Vernunfterkenntnis von denkenden Wesen überhaupt mehr, als das *cogito* zum Grunde...so würde eine empirische Psychologie entspringen.

But in this process the proposition *I think* is taken only problematically. I.e., it is not taken insofar as it may contain a perception of an existent (the Cartesian *cogito, ergo sum*); the proposition is taken, rather, in terms of its mere possibility, in order to see what properties may from so simple a proposition flow to its subject (whether or not such a subject exists). If our pure rational cognition of thinking beings as such were based on more than the *cogito*...then there would arise an empirical psychology. (386)

Leaving aside the remarkable selection of pronouns (*Ich, Er, Es*), one can see that Kant performs one operation in the guise of another. He attributes to Descartes a normalization of the statement "*cogito*" or "I think" in order to make it into the name of an auto-referential operation by which thought takes itself for its own object, the complete formula of which would be: "I am cognizant of the fact that I think that I think." He designates as "subject" (*subjectum* translated by him as *Subjekt*), in the classical metaphysical sense, the "something" or the "being" that exists simultaneously as that which is aiming and aimed at by thought (as the pole or support of the attribution of predicates). Thus Kant suggests to his successors (Fichte and Hegel) that the only conceivable subject (*hupokeimenon*) is one that thinks itself and its own predicates, which are its thoughts. From a Cartesian point of view, these two operations are contradictory, as will be clear if one rereads the *Meditations*. Strictly speaking, the nominalization of the simple phrase "*cogito*" cannot be found in Descartes, even if it is anticipated by the way he reflects on the properties of his own statement. On the other hand, the move toward the metaphysical subject is, properly speaking, incompatible with the *cogito*, which in the *Meditations* is reduced to the existential proposition, "I am, I exist." The *cogito* is inseparable from a first-person enunciation (*ego*) to which Descartes opposes the "He" (*Il, Ille*) of God and the "this" (*ceci, hoc*) of the body. "I think" is equivalent to "I am," which is developed as "I am what I am," that is to say, I am my soul (*mens*), not Him (God), or this (my body). Clearly, we are faced with a misinterpretation with rather serious consequences, since the whole of transcendental philosophy up to Husserl and Heidegger read Descartes through Kant's eyes and thus ceaselessly reproached Descartes for having "substantialized the subject" at the very moment of its discovery.

This misinterpretation, however, is fundamentally a result of the difficulty encountered by Kant in trying to situate a revolutionary idea in which all the originality of his "transcendental dialectics" is concentrated, an idea that is as different from the "subjectivity" of Aristotelian metaphysics as it is from the "ipseity" of the Cartesian "thinking thing" (*ego ipse a me percipior*): the idea of the truth of perceptive appearance inherent to thought. For Kant, we are not capable of thinking without our inner sense being affected by thinking itself and, consequently, without the emergence of an illusion of an "inner reality" (itself an object of thought). Hence, the think-ing "I" recognizes itself in its logical function precisely to the degree that it cannot help but misrecognize itself by believing that it is knowable as a phenomenon, taken literally as "that which appears" in the scene of representation (*erscheint*). The substance, for Kant, is no longer of the order of being or of "the thing in itself," but rather it is only the concept of that which remains permanent in phenomena. The subject, as a power or faculty of logic, is not substantial since it is not phenomenal; however, inasmuch as it thinks (itself), it *appears* in the modality of a substance. In the "Transcendental Deduction," Kant writes, "Accordingly I have no *cognition* of myself as I am but merely cognition of how I appear to myself (*wie ich mich selbst erscheine*)" (196). The "I" — which is only given in the form of an inseparable statement "I think" that also functions as its proper, that is to say, generic, "name" — is only capable of apprehending itself (and thereby also "affecting" itself) in an illusory manner. But this illusion or transcendental appearance (*Schein*) is the only one to deliver an original verity: it is the only possible form of a foundation. In a certain sense, it is truth itself. "Subject" is the word that henceforth denotes this amazing unity of contraries and Kant attributes to Descartes this metaphysical illusion of which he claims to have freed himself. By making this "mistake," Descartes bears witness to the fact that truth lies at the heart of illusion.

In all this — in which the syntactic forms of enunciation and translations or transpositions play a crucial role — it seems that we have to deal exclusively with epistemological propositions and experiences of thought. The *a fortiori* "practical," political dimension of the question of the subject is never addressed explicitly. Nevertheless, the certainty of this observation might be questioned if one pays attention to two features of the argument that I want to focus on here. The first complication is that the Kantian subject (that is, the *Ich* or, better still, the *Ich denke*) is fundamentally given in a relation of *reflection*. This provides for the subject — that is to say, the subject attributes to itself — a representation that is at the same time truth and error, recognition and misrecognition. The second observation is that this circle of apperception opens onto an *injunction* which the subject is not only tempted but also required to approach through the form of the categorical imperative itself: the injunction of liberating its own representation from "phenomenalism" (or from substantialism, which amounts to the same thing) in order to attach it to the idea of a "pure" activity of thought. Such an idea has no meaning within the horizon of nature; it can only take on meaning as the correlate of liberty. It is at this point that the way the argument of the "Paralogism of Pure Reason" proceeds — by way of identifying the transcendental "subject" (or the reflexive identity of the "I" [*Selbst*]) with the moral personality (*Persönlichkeit*), which renders the human being "capable of being the citizen of a better world than he thinks" — acquires its full significance.

Historically speaking, we would like to be able to relate this substratum of Kantian thought to the "becoming subject" of the revolutionary and post-revolutionary citizen and, notably, to the constitution of the category of the "subject of right" (*Rechtssubjekt*). In a recent study, Yves-Charles Zarka — opposing a version of justice and equality that demands that each subject place itself in the place of all others — identifies Leibniz as the source of the emergence of the expression *subjectum juris*, referring to a universalizing "moral quality" of its bearer.[3] But we also know that even though Kant, like Hegel, might seem to be the closest to defining the divisions of right, he himself never used the expression "subject of right," for which, it appears, one would have to turn to the historical school of right (Savigny, Hugo, Puchta). These subjects (*Subjekte*), in relation to which one thinks of "obligation," have nothing to do with political "subjects" (*Untertan*, Kant's equivalent of the Latin *subditus*) obeying a *sovereign* (which could be the people itself in the form of a state). The encounter with the themes of sovereignty and law, which implicitly invoke the ideas of the liberation of the subject and of the subject as that "which liberates itself," thus remains repressed.

SUBJECTUS/SUBJECTUM: THE HISTORICAL PLAY OF WORDS

Since they refer to this double etymology, the French *su(b)jet*, the English *subject*, the Spanish *sujeto*, and the Italian *soggetto* make immediately apparent what the German word *Subjekt*, because of its difference from *Untertan*, is not capable of evoking: on the one hand, they refer to *subjectum*, meaning the agent of individual properties; on the other hand, they also refer to *subjectus*, meaning subjugated to law or power. In other words, we are dealing with the problems of presupposition and subjection: the negotiation of the gap between the term aimed at by the question "who?" and that aimed at by the question "what?" We maintain that this linguistic difference played a crucial role in the formation of Western philosophy, and thus spoke of this subject (parodying certain French translations of Heidegger) as a historical play of words, the effects of which could be traced from Hobbes to Foucault (by way of Rousseau, Hegel, Nietzsche, and Bataille).

"Subject" was not originally one of the "words of opposing meaning" that so fascinated Freud, but it did become one, in the sense that liberty and constraint now appear as two sides of the same coin. The origins of this overdetermination cannot be found in Greek, even when one makes an analogy with the construction of the terms *hupokeimenon* (the substratum or the support), *hypostasis* (the foundation or substance, before becoming the technical term designating the persons of the Trinity), and *hypèkoos* ("he who obeys to the speech": the servant, the disciple, the vassal paying a tribute). We have to turn instead to Latin — that is, to imperial and Christian Rome — and then to the history of theologico-politics and moral anthropology centered around obedience as the road to salvation.

The development of *subjectus* as a juristic figure extends over seventeen centuries, from Roman Law to absolute monarchy. The first question that emerges is: how do you move from the enumeration of individuals subjugated to the power of another to the representation of the human race as a community of "subjects"? The distinction between independent and dependent persons was the foundation of Roman Law. Suffice it to recall a text by Gaius: "Next comes another division in the law of persons. For some persons are *sui iuris* (independent) and others are *alieni iuris* (dependent on another). Again, of those *alieni iuris* some are in *potestas* [in power], others in *manus* [in hand, under the jurisdiction of another], and others in *mancipium* [enslaved]. Let us consider first persons *alieni iuris*; for, knowing these, we shall at the same time know who are *sui iuris*."[4] As we can see, it is by the dialectical division of the forms of subjection (*assujettissement*) that one obtains the definition of the free man, the master; however, for this division to create a link between subjects, the notions of *potestas*, *manus*, and *mancipium* are not sufficient. What is needed is an *imperium* (absolute authority). An idea of universal subjection only appears with the empire, in relation to the person of the emperor to whom the citizens and many of the non-citizens owe "service," *officium*. This condition, however, is still not sufficient: it is necessary that the Romans could be submitted to *imperium* in the *same manner* (if that was ever a possibility) as the conquered populations, the so-called "subjects of the Roman people" — a confusion that, contradictorily, points toward the horizon of the generalized Roman citizenship as personal status within the empire. And above all, it is necessary that the *imperium* be founded theologically as a Christian *imperium*, a spiritual power issuing from God and conserved by him, reigning not only over the body but over (and in) the soul as well.

The subject taken in this sense (the "subject of law" or *sujet du droit*) is the absolute opposite of what was later called the "subject of right" (*sujet de droit, Rechtssubjekt*). Its major characteristic is that it is a *subditus* (subordinate) but not a *servus* (slave). Calling the subject *subditus* means that it enters a relation of obedience. Obedience is not established only between a ruler who has the right to constrain and those submitted to this power, but also between a *sublimis* (one "elected" to command) and the *subditi* or *subjecti* (those who turn to him to receive the law). The power to constrain is distributed along a hierarchy of powers. Obedience is the principle that makes the obedient into members of the same body. Obedience itself, concentrated at the top in the figure of a *principium/princeps*, fundamentally still comes from below; as *subditi*, the subjects *want* their own proper obedience to be inscribed into the economy of creation and salvation. Thus, knowing that all power comes from God, the *faithful one who happens to be a subject* [*fidèle sujet*] is also necessarily a *faithful subject* [*sujet fidèle*].

With its unity of principle and its numberless forms, such an obedience implies a notion of the soul that was unknown to antiquity, or at least was not used in the same way to think a political relation. For an ancient Greek, it is not the soul that obeys. Obedience is a contingent situation in which one finds oneself in relation to a commander (*arkhon*), but this relation also provides (at least in a democratic *politeia*) that one can become a commander oneself, which is the Aristotelian definition of the citizen. This notion of obedience, then, is a natural dependence of the domestic type. From this perspective, the concept of "free obedience" is a contradiction in terms. It is quite significant that the idea that a slave could *also* be free only comes later (with Stoicism): on a *different* level (in a "cosmic" city, a city of "souls") those who are slaves here may be masters (of themselves, of their passions), and they can also be citizens tied to others by a reciprocal link (*philia*). There is nothing here that would even approximate an idea of liberty residing in obedience and that would be a result of this obedience itself. In order to conceive of that, the idea of obedience has to be transferred to the side of the soul and must no longer be thought of as natural: it has to name a supernatural part of the individual that understands the divinity of order.

The *subditus-subjectus* was constantly distinguished from the slave, in the same way that the sovereignty of the prince, the *sublimes*, was distinguished from despotism, which is literally the authority of a master of slaves. But this fundamental distinction was elaborated in different ways. Within the theological tradition, the subject is a believer, a Christian, which could mean that since it is his soul that obeys, he will never be a "thing" owned by the sovereign; his obedience corresponds to the responsibility or duty of the prince. This manner of thinking the liberty of the subject, however, is in practice extraordinarily ambivalent: the subject can either understand itself as an affirmation and active contribution of its will to obedience (just as the Christian, by his works, "cooperates in his salvation"), or as an annihilation of the will — this is why the mystics try to annihilate themselves in the contemplation of God, the only absolute sovereign. Autonomy dwells with nothingness, "propriety" with "de-propriation."

It is nevertheless evident that when the return of the "citizen" gets underway in medieval and renaissance villages, it does not allow itself to be reduced to *zôion politikon*: Thomas Aquinas, who translates the expression as "social animal," distinguishes man's *christianitas* (a supernatural quality) from his *humanitas* (something natural), that is, he distinguishes "believer" from "citizen." So what happens to the "subject" here? In a certain sense, it is more autonomous insofar as its subjection is the effect of a political order that integrates "civility" and "politics," and inscribes itself into nature. But it becomes ever more difficult to conceive of it as *subditus*: the concept of its essential obedience is threatened. This contradiction erupts in the absolute monarchy that takes the mysterious unity of the "two bodies" of the temporal and the spiritual sovereign to its final extreme. The same goes for the liberty of the subject. There is only one prince whose will is law, who is "father of his subjects," and has absolute authority over them: "*L'État, c'est moi*," as Louis XIV said. Yet the absolute monarchy is precisely a power of *the State*, that is to say, a power that institutes and exercises itself by law and administration. Thus, its subjects are, if not "subjects of right," at least subjects "in right," members of a republic (what Hobbes called the Commonwealth). *The subjects are the citizens.* Or, as Jean Bodin explains, "[w]e can say then that every citizen is a subject since his liberty is limited by the sovereign power to which he owes obedience. We cannot say that every subject is a citizen. This is clear from the case of slaves."[5] Under the given circumstances, however, this does not render untenable the condition of the citizen as the "free subject who is dependent on the sovereignty of another."[6] Boethius, by a reversal of terms, opposes to these theories the definition of the power of the One as a "voluntary servitude" on which the reason of the State does not confer any meaning of supernatural liberty. The controversy over the (non-)difference between absolutism and despotism accompanies the whole history of absolute monarchy. And from the point of view of the new citizen and its revolution (which will also be an essential source of its own idealization), the condition of the subject will be retrospectively identified with that of the slave, the subjection into slavery.

SUBJECTIVITY *à la française*

Now it is possible to interpret how contemporary philosophy — especially that written in French — understands the question of subjectivity: not as a question of essence, relating being to truth and appearance, or to the opposition between nature and liberty as in the metaphysical tradition, but *as a political question*, as a becoming or relation of forces themselves "internal" to their conflicts.

From the point of view of the history of ideas and words, it would be helpful to have at our disposal a certain number of intermediary links that we will mention only in passing here. First and foremost, there are the two faces of Rousseau's oeuvre and the corresponding *tours d'écriture* that left an omnipresent trace. Think of the way the *Social Contract* presents the citizen (which is a part of the sovereignty, that is, author of the law) and the subject (which finds its liberty in absolute obedience to the same law) as strict correlatives due to the "total alienation" of individual wills that functions as the source of a general will. This general will in turn constitutes a "communal I" reflected by all the individual consciousnesses, as Hegel wrote in the *Phenomenology of Spirit* (implicitly referring to Rousseau): "an I that is a we and a we that is an I." Keep in mind, however, the way his autobiographical writings associate the theme of the authenticity of the "I" with that of subjectivation: "There is not a day when I do not remember with joy and tenderness this unique and brief time of my life, when I was fully myself, without mixture and without obstacle, and when I can truly say I lived…I could not endure subjection [*assujettissement*]; I was perfectly free, and more than free, because, subjected by my attachment alone, I only did what I wished to do."[7]

Furthermore, one would have to take into consideration the effects of the revolutionary break that cannot be restricted merely to the "sublation" of the subject (*subjectus, subditus*) by the citizen (entitled to political rights), since it also carries out a becoming subject (*subjectum*) of the citizen. This process involves a naturalization of his or her humanity, which inscribes all anthropological differences (age, sex, culture, health, capabilities, morality, and so on) into an "individual character" that determines its social recognition and with which it (more or less) identifies itself in the course of its education. This shift forms the historical and political conditions of possibility of the subversion of the relation between sovereignty and subjectivity. Such would be (at least according to our hypothesis) the genealogy of the identification of the *problem of subjectivity* and the *problem of subjection* that completely transforms the meaning of the question of the subject in philosophy (and at the same time our perception of its history).

As a final note, let's look at two thinkers who bring the question of the subject up to the present moment. It is Lacan and Foucault who, although in very different ways, employ the specter of subjectivity in the most systematic manner as the process of subjection. Lacan recollects this distant heritage by reference to two paradoxical but absolutely idiomatic French phrases: "the I is detestable" ("*le moi est haissable*" — Pascal) and "I am an other" ("*Je est un autre*" — Rimbaud). What is the subject for him? Nothing but the succession of effects of a living individual's alienation from the "law of the signifier": if it has to be taken as irreducible, the subject is never originary, but always already "dependent." It only exists as a returning effect of the speech that constitutes it (and names it in the first place) in a symbolic universe of discourses and institutions that are, by definition, impossible to master. Lacan interprets the "lack of knowledge" constitutive of the unconscious precisely in these terms. Because it is submitted to the signifier that irreparably separates it from itself, the subject infinitely oscillates between the illusion of identity (the narcissistic beliefs of an "imaginary captation" summarized by the figure of the "I") and the unknown element involved in the conflict (the recognition of a question coming from the *other* [primarily the other sex] as that which is nevertheless most properly its own). This is, no doubt, the choice that constitutes the subject: "if desire is an effect in the subject of the condition that is imposed on him by the existence of the discourse, to make his need pass through the defiles of the signifier...the subject has to find the constituting structure of his desire in the same gap opened up by the effect of the signifiers in those who come to represent the Other for him, in so far as his demand is subjected to them."[8] At best, analysis reverses the course of the constitution of desire that leads the subject back to the enunciation of its "lack in being"; as Lacan points out, "[d]esire merely subjects what analysis makes subjective."[9]

Foucault, in turn, found the model of the relationship between subjectivity, appearance, and truth in the methods of obtaining and providing confessions (passed on from religion and inquisition to psychology and psychiatry). Furthermore, in Bentham's panopticism, he found the ideal diagram of all "fictitious relations," materialized in the play of the institutions of social normalization, from which a "real subjection is born mechanically."[10] Starting from here, he created the program of an investigation of the modes of objectification that transform human beings into subjects and, most notably, of power relations. But there is no power, neither over the self nor over others, that does not proceed by way of the constitution of a certain knowledge. Therefore, this knowledge is not simply a theoretical activity, but a social practice, a production of objectivity. The questions of the subject and of the object — understood as a double process of subjectivation and objectivation, the subjectivation of the individual by rules and the construction of the "relation of self to self" according to different practical modalities — are not opposed to one another, but are two sides of the same reality. "Still within the framework of the same general project, Michel Foucault has now attempted to study the constitution of the subject as object for itself: the formation of the procedures by which the subject is driven to observe, analyze, decipher, and recognize itself as a domain of possible knowledge. In short, he is dealing with the history of 'subjectivity' — if one understands by this word the manner in which the subject experiences itself in a game of truth where it has a relation to itself."[11] The very words of the "transcendental dialectics" turned against their original meaning! We can identify here a circle of presuppositions: the subject is the aggregate of the apparatuses of subjection or subjectivation that act objectively upon the "subjectivity" of the individual; that is to say, they presuppose the "liberty" of the subject or a capacity to resist in order to turn this subjectivity against itself. In other words, we are dealing with a differential of power that simultaneously opens up the possibility of a politics (attempting to liberate the individual from certain modes of discipline and from certain types of individuality) and of an ethics (inventing new relations of power and "practices of liberty" that are modes of access rather than of self-consciousness).

These propositions, in their conflicting dispersion, transform our reading of European history. By conferring the light of evidence on the associations and metaphors that underlie Nietzsche's text, they make possible another use of the subjectivity defined by the *Critique of Pure Reason*. If the subject (*subjectum, Subjekt*, but also *subjectus*) had not been placed in an internal relation with personal subjection and therefore with political, juristic, and theological power (of which that subject is the effect and inverse image), we would not be able to recognize in the paradoxical conjunction of truth and transcendental appearances discussed in the "Paralogisms of Pure Reason" the sign of an originary difference (or *différance*) that redirects us to the ethics of internal obedience and ascetism rather than to the metaphysics of spirit and the psychology of "self consciousness." In the end, these propositions reopen the question of the active finitude that defines the Cartesian subject (or non-subject): but not so much as "nature" or thinking "substance," that is to say, as *representation*, but as a *revindication* (as Canguilhem would say) of a power to say "I," "between the infinite and nothing," or between God and the body.

Translated by Roland Végső

This selection is a partial translation of the entry "Subject," written by Etienne Balibar for the *Vocabulaire Européen des Philosophies*, directed by Barbara Cassin and forthcoming from Éditions du Seuil and Le Robert.

1. Friedrich Nietzsche, *Beyond Good and Evil: Prelude to a Philosophy of the Future*, ed. Rolf-Peter Horstmann and Judith Norman, trans. Judith Norman (Cambridge: Cambridge University Press, 2002), 18-20. [Balibar cites the following French edition of Nietzsche's text: *Par delà bien et mal* in *Œuvres philosophiques complètes*, vol. 7, ed. Giorgio Colli and Mazzino Montinari, trans. C. Heim, I. Hildenbrandt, and J. Gratien (Paris: Gallimard, 1971). I quote from the latest English edition and provide this French translation and the original German text in brackets where necessary. Trans.]

2. Immanuel Kant, *Critique of Pure Reason*, trans. Werner S. Pluhar (Indianapolis: Hackett, 1996), 177; brackets in the original. Subsequent references will appear parenthetically within the text. For the German text, see Kant, *Kritik der reinen Vernunft* (Hamburg: Felix Meiner, 1956).

3. See Yves-Charles Zarka, "L'invention du sujet de droit," in *Archives de philosophie* 60 (1997): 531-550.

4. Gaius, *The Institutes of Gaius. Part I*, trans. Francis de Zulueta (Oxford: Clarendon, 1946), 17.

5. Jean Bodin, *Six Books of the Commonwealth*, trans. M. J. Tooley (New York: Barnes and Noble, 1967), 19.

6. Ibid.

7. Jean-Jacques Rousseau, *The Reveries of a Solitary*, trans. John Gould Fletcher (New York: Brentano, 1927), 194-195.

8. Jacques Lacan, *Écrits: A Selection*, trans. Alan Sheridan (New York: Norton, 1977), 264.

9. Ibid., 260.

10. Michel Foucault, *Discipline and Punish: The Birth of the Prison*, trans. Alan Sheridan (New York: Pantheon, 1979), 202.

11. Foucault, "Foucault," in *Dits et écrits, 1954-1988* (Paris: Éditions Gallimard, 1994), 4:633. [Editor's translation.]

OMNITUDO REALITATIS
marina de carneri

I say that just as we cannot move freely without taking hold the ground, and since we cannot take hold the ground without moving freely, so we cannot make use of reason unless we freely believe and we cannot believe unless we make use of reason.

— Franz von Baader[1]

If we want to re-insert ethics into our system of thought, we will have to address the question of finality and its subject with the awareness that in a time and culture that is committed exclusively to the recognition of the physical incidence of any event, a truly ethical act will tend to go unrecognized or, at the very least, be misunderstood. A dangerous situation. For if the erasure of the ethical plane continues long and consistently enough   and this is a possibility clearly indicated by Kant at the end of a short essay entitled "The End of All Things" — then "from a moral point of view the (perverse) *end of all things* would make its entrance."[2] Kant calls this, without mincing his words, the advent of the Antichrist.

But let's go back to the argument of the essay itself, which is an exploration of the way in which the idea of a *telos*, of an end of all things, has to be thought from the point of view of reason. The first thing to note is that the question can be approached only from the point of view of ethics, that is, from the point of view of a God conceived exclusively as a necessary function of reason. This means that ethics coincides with a "religion" that addresses each and every human being as a subject of reason and therefore as a being inherently capable of distinguishing good from evil. Kant identifies this universal religion with Christianity insofar as Christianity is the religion of love, where love is the manifestation of the respect for "the law, which, as an unchangeable order that lies in the nature of things, does not leave it up even to the Creator's will to decide whether its consequences will be thus or otherwise."[3]

The problem, however, is to determine how to think about a law inherent to the end of all things, for it is evident that such a law cannot coincide with the laws that are laid down by science. Scientific laws, predicated on the delimitation of a clear field of observation, are simply descriptions of the apparent functioning of things. In order to address the idea of a law of things themselves, it is necessary to think in terms of ends, that is, in terms of time and eternity. The dimension of the ethical can be philosophically proven to exist as a necessary law only if the idea of eternity can be shown to be an idea inherent to reason itself. In that case, a type of act can be conceived whose end is not the relative or the arbitrary, but the absolutely valid and the eternally true. It is the question of eternity that Kant's "The End of All Things" addresses:

> It is a common expression, especially when speaking piously, for a dying man to say that he is *passing from time into eternity.*

> In fact, this expression would mean nothing if by "eternity" one were to understand the infinite passage of time; for then man would surely never emerge from time, but would always only pass from one moment of time to another. Thus, by this expression must be meant the *end of all time* in man's uninterrupted survival, though we nonetheless mean by this duration (of his existence considered as a quantity) a quantity (*duratio noumenon*) that is utterly incomparable to time, and we surely cannot have any (but a merely negative) concept of it. This thought contains something a bit horrifying, for it leads to an abyss, from which there is no possible return for whosoever falls into it...[Y]et it also contains something appealing, for one cannot cease from returning one's frightened eyes to it...It is frightfully-*sublime*, in part because of its obscurity, by which the imagination is made more powerfully active than by bright light. Finally, it must be interwoven into universal human reason in a wonderful way, for it is found in one guise or another among all reasoning peoples in all times. Now since we follow this passage out of time into eternity (whether this idea has objective reality or not), it may, from a theoretical point of view, be considered to extend cognitive knowledge in a moral context, just as when reason itself makes this passage, we come up against the *end of all things* as a [form of] temporal being and as an object of possible experience.[4]

Why is thinking about the end of time so vital that there is no place or culture that has not addressed the question? The reason is that the thought of an end both in the sense of termination and of final meaning is a law internal to thought itself. Insofar as it is predicated on the articulation of concepts according to the principle of non-contradiction, rational thinking both takes place in time and is constitutive of time. Time, therefore, represents the very limit of thought, and by thinking time, thought attempts to go beyond itself. This is the reason why, as Kant says, the thought of the end of time is "terrible and sublime at the same time," and it can be better approached by imagination than by reason itself. In fact, to pursue the thought of the end of time means to bring about the suicide of reason. If reason must be replaced in this task by imagination, then we must conceive of a different type of imagination, namely one that does not form images, for images are still representations of thoughts. Let's say then that the end of time can be grasped neither by reason, nor by imagination, but by intuition. But how can we grasp the value of such intuition? Is it a logical intuition of the negation of the concept of time, or is it the real thing, that is, the perception of the infinite in a glimpse? In any case, the notion of an end of all things is predicated on the possibility of this intuition, and ethics can only come into being from the idea that things have an end. Kant writes: "in the moral order of purposes, this end [of time] is at the same time the beginning of the *supersensuous* survival of these same temporal beings, consequently the beginning of their existence as beings that do not stand under conditions of time, and thus their beginning as beings whose state is such as to allow nothing other than a moral evaluation [*Bestimmung*] of their nature."[5] Thus, the destination of things in themselves is the accomplishment of their nature according to their own inherent law — the ultimate law — and ethics is constituted as the pursuit of this order. The question is whether or not the mind can have a view of this order by way of the intuition of infinity.

Kant addresses this problem in the *Critique of Pure Reason* and concludes that the intuition of infinity is not the direct apprehension of the order of things in themselves, but rather the moment in which reason apprehends itself as reason. Let's backtrack and see how he comes to this conclusion. The section entitled "On the Transcendental Ideal" opens:

> Every *concept* is, as regards what is not contained in this concept itself, indeterminate and subject to the principle of *determinability*: viz., that of *every two* predicates contradictorily opposed to each other only one can belong to the concept. This principle rests on the principle of contradiction, and hence is a merely logical principle that abstracts from all content of cognition and has in view nothing but the cognition's logical form.

> But every *thing* is, with regard to its possibility, subject also to the principle of *thoroughgoing determination*, whereby of *all possible* predicates of *things*, insofar as these predicates are compared with their opposites, one must belong to the thing. This principle rests not merely on the principle of contradiction. For besides considering the relation of two predicates that conflict with each other, the principle considers every thing also in relation to *possibility in its entirety*.[6]

The formation of concepts is made possible by two principles of reason. The first is the principle of non-contradiction, according to which a concept cannot be defined by two predicates that contradict each other. The second is the principle of thoroughgoing determination that defines a thing in relation to all its possible predicates because in order to cognize a thing completely we must presuppose an indeterminate number of possible attributes whose existence we must verify. At the end of this thoroughgoing determination, we will be able to say that we know the thing. Thus, as Kant points out in a note to the same section, the determinability of a concept through the principle of non-contradiction is based on the universality (*universalitas*) of the principle of the excluded middle between two opposing predicates. But the very possibility of this determinability is in turn based on the presupposition of the sum of all possible predicates of a thing, that is, on the presupposition of the thing as a set made up of an indeterminate number of attributes (*universitas*).[7] In other words, the idea of the whole as the locus of infinity has to be posited by reason *before* the determination of the predicates that qualify a thing. Kant calls the notion of the whole "the transcendental substratum in our reason" and says that this substratum provides the idea of the *totality of reality — omnitudo realitatis*. He concludes that "a transcendental *ideal* is what underlies the thoroughgoing determination found necessarily with everything that exists, and this ideal is what amounts to the supreme and complete material condition of the possibility of everything that exists — the condition to which all thinking of objects as such as regards their content must be traced back."[8]

What is important to point out here is that the transcendental ideal — the presupposition of the notion of the whole — is not itself an object of experience, but an object of reason, that is, it is the *a priori* condition for the perception of any actual object of experience. In this sense, it is not the thing in itself, but rather what Kant calls the *noumenon*, that which provides the rational ground for the perception of the thing as we know it (*phenomenon*). The transcendental ideal is therefore the groundless ground of reason because reason does not presuppose the existence of a being that conforms to this ideal. Thus, "the ideal is for reason the archetype (*prototypon*) of all things, the things which one and all — as deficient copies (*ectypa*) — take the material for their possibility from that archetype, and which while approximating it either more or less are nonetheless always infinitely far from attaining it."[9] With the formulation of the transcendental ideal, Kant brings the faculty of reason to its limit and to a paradox: through the idea of totality, reason indeed founds itself, but *only as reason, not as reality*, because totality, being the infinite set of all possible attributes, cannot be an object of direct cognition without immediately nullifying the principle of the excluded middle. The notion of totality, therefore, is not a concept, but simply a regulative idea of reason. The paradox of this formulation lies in the fact that we are thereby led to think the unthinkable as unthinkable and to conclude that the ineffable is the very essence and source of reason. As a result — and to return to the original question — the intuition of infinity, according to Kant, is not the intuition of something infinitely real, that is, of God as being, or the thing in itself, but is the intuition of the *noumenon*, that is, of the infinite productivity of reason.

But how does this sit with the idea of an end of all things, which is based, Kant says, on the law inherent in things themselves? Can ethics, unlike knowledge, be based on the intuition of the thing itself? Kant excludes the possibility of accessing the realm of ends once more in the moment in which he lays down the foundations of practical reason. In the *Fundamental Principles of the Metaphysic of Morals*, he writes, "if the critique of a pure practical reason is to be complete, it must be possible at the same time to show its identity with the speculative reason in a common principle, for it can ultimately be only one and the same reason which has to be distinguished merely in its application."[10] How is this identity demonstrated? The coincidence between pure practical and speculative reason lies in the fact that man, insofar as he is a rational being, has the faculty to act according to the conception of laws, that is, the faculty to discern the functioning of the law and, as a consequence, the will to act correspondingly. In other words, for Kant, to perceive the law means to *want* to listen to its command and implies feeling the imperative to obey it. He asks, "whence have we the conception of God as the supreme good? Simply from the *idea* of moral perfection, which reason frames *a priori*, and connects inseparably with the notion of a free-will."[11] Thus, the will is free insofar as it *freely* realizes the law without objecting to it. It is evident, however, that if the law needs to *speak* (in the form of an imperative), it is because something on the other end *does not want to listen*. Moral perfection seems to be, then, something that may never take place in reality. But this does not undermine its necessity and validity from the point of view of reason because what can be conceived can and must be performed, at least in infinity. What is important to stress is that the Kantian God, from the point of view of practical reason, where it identifies with the good, does not coincide with the supreme being, but with *the thinking of it*. If the divine or holy will is the will that does not obey the categorical imperative, because *it is* the categorical imperative, still the law that the divine will articulates is a law of reason, not a law of being. Further, the moral act of identifying the good with God — that is, with the totality of the universe as substance — would be, as Kant says in the *Critique of Pure Reason*, a "transcendental subreption" because it would be mistaking the concept of a thing for the thing in itself.

But what exactly is the thing in itself? We could say that it is a terminus, a concept that indicates both itself and its beyond. On the one hand, it is simply the unity that thought must presuppose behind each concept of reason, and in this sense it is the cause of all the predicates that we attribute to the things in the world. On the other hand, it points to the material origin of all possible predicates that is completely inaccessible to reason, and therefore nothing can be said about it. The thing in itself as the origin of all possible predicates is to be thought of as God. And Kant concludes, "the supreme being remains for the merely speculative use of reason a mere *ideal* — but yet a *faultless* ideal, a concept that concludes and crowns the whole of human cognition. Although the concept's objective reality cannot be proved by this speculative path, it also cannot be refuted by it."[12] Just as the *phenomenon* is constituted by the *noumenon* and the thing in itself, so the idea of God appears twice, first as an ideal of reason and secondly as the ideal's objective reality that we can neither prove nor disprove.

To recapitulate, in the Kantian system we find three orders: the *phenomenon*, what we experience sensually; the *noumenon*, that which *allows* us to think what we experience; and the thing in itself, about which absolutely nothing can be said because we always apprehend it in a mediated form, either *by experience* as *phenomenon*, or *intellectually* as *noumenon*. What Kant discounts is the idea that something of the thing in itself must enter the *phenomenon* if the order of experience is to exist at all. Kant affords a primary role to experience because he recognizes that a concept has no value unless it either derives from experience or is applicable to it. This means that at the origin of reason there is sensibility, and nothing that is not first in sensibility can be articulated by reason. Nevertheless, for Kant experience exists as such only because of the mediation of the categories of the understanding: "the understanding can a priori never accomplish more than to anticipate the form of a possible experience as such; and since what is not appearance cannot be an object of experience, the understanding can never overstep the limits of sensibility within which alone objects are given to us."[13]

Walter Benjamin has observed that this notion of experience is not unique to Kant, but belongs to the philosophical tradition preceding him. We can reformulate it like this: according to tradition, experience and knowledge coincide. There can be experience only if an object is isolated and turned into a concept. Since reason is the function of thinking that is in charge of the production of concepts, there is no experience without reason. Benjamin points out in relation to Kant, however, that experience (*Erfahrung*) is not the same as knowledge (*Erkenntnis*).[14] What type of experience brings no knowledge of an object? Can we still call it experience? And who is experiencing what? If we continue to follow Kant's analysis, we come to a crucial moment in the construction of experience. The understanding organizes sensibility around the transcendental ideal, that is, around the projection of totality, which allows the perception of things as units. Since what defines a unit is the fact that it can be repeated infinitely, Kant concludes that sensibility is intrinsically temporal and that the perception of things takes place *in the temporal mode of the present, which is the never-ending repetition of the instant of totality as the matrix that attracts all the predicates belonging to a thing*:

> No one can explicate the concept of magnitude as such, except perhaps by saying that it is that determination of a thing whereby we can think how many times a unit is posited in it. Yet this how-many-times is based on successive repetition, and hence on time and the synthesis (of the homogeneous) in time. Reality contrasted with negation can be explicated only if one thinks of a time (as the sum of all being) that is either filled with something or empty. If from the concept of substance I omit permanence (which is an existence at all time), then *I have nothing left for this concept but the logical presentation of subject*, a presentation that I mean to realize by presenting something *that can occur only as subject (i.e., only without being a predicate of anything)*. However, not only do I not know any conditions at all under which some thing will possess this logical superiority; but we also cannot make from it anything further, and cannot draw from it the least inference. For through this explication no object whatever is determined for the use of the concept of substance, and hence *we do not know at all whether the concept in fact signifies anything whatsoever*.[15]

How are we to think the instant in and through which the idea of unity can be realized? Kant observes that it cannot be thought of as substance, but as a concept it signifies nothing whatsoever. We can conceive of it only as a discontinuity between sensibility and understanding, something that, Kant says, can occur only as subject because it has no attributes, and yet is the condition for all the attributes to appear. Kant calls the moment of the synthesis of the homogeneous in time "subject" because in itself it has no attributes and therefore no signification. Since it has no attributes, it also cannot be thought of as substance, so Kant admits that he can make no more of it. But we can.

The subject as the temporal pulsation of the form of totality is what allows for the constitution of both the *noumenon* and the *phenomenon*. It is the moment of pure experience that allows the taking place of experience as knowledge of an object. In this sense, it is the moment in which *something of the thing in itself is communicated to the understanding as something that is not of the same order*. The subject is *not simply a logical moment*, as Kant seems to think, but is the moment of *pure experience without an object that cannot be itself an object of experience because it is pure pathos*. Thus, at the origin of knowledge as a product of the understanding there is a moment in which the thing in itself appears as subject, and its mode of being is not *logos* (reason as language), but *pathos*. I use the term pathos to indicate that modality of experience which, because it is not organized around an object (that is, through language), remains *unconscious* and must be understood as *pure affect* without any connotations. Moreover, the subject defined in this way coincides with time as infinity because it precedes the differentiation of past, present, and future, which is an effect of thinking. *Time is the subject*. The subject as pathos is the infinite repetition of the now, a repetition which, being prior to signification, cannot be thought as repetition either of the same or of the different, but as the recurrence of the *absolutely singular*. Absolute singularity is the pre-reflective point at which internal and external, language and experience, ego and object, past and future coincide and disappear.

The subject as pathos is thus not the same as the transcendental subject, which is simply a regulative ideal of reason, nor is it an object of reason posited by reason itself, like the Cartesian cogito. The subject as temporality does not configure itself in opposition to an object, which is not to say that the moment of the relation between subject and object does not exist. The subject in relation to an object is not the *real* subject as temporality; rather, it is an ego that is constituted by the object that it happens to address. We must therefore distinguish between the subject, which is beyond signification, and the ego, which results from the type of relation entered into with an object, and can be made an object of thought and of consciousness. It is the ego that Descartes discovered as the subject of the cogito. Kant clarifies the essence of the cogito: "I am conscious of my existence as determined in time. All time determination presupposes something *permanent* in perception. But this permanent something cannot be something within me, precisely because my existence can be determined in time only by this permanent something. Therefore perception of this permanent something is possible only through a *thing* outside me...Hence determination of my existence in time is possible only through the existence of actual things that I perceive outside me."[16] As a result, we can say that the ego catches itself thinking and makes itself into an object, that is, into a *res cogitans*. Moreover, because the ego as object of the cogito is formed by its relation to an object of experience, its identity is essentially unstable as it depends on the object itself. Consequently, the operation of self-reflection with the correlative production of a *res cogitans*, although necessary, can never be fulfilled in its entirety precisely because the cogito will never be able to coincide with the unstoppable flight of ego experiences.

Let us now return to the question of the end. For Kant, the end of all things is forever external to reason, but reason can approximate it through the assumption of the notion of the totality of reality, that is, through the transcendental ideal. This means that reason is constitutively unable to enter the kingdom of ends, even though it functions as a guide in that it indicates the direction an act must take in order to be ethical. However, an absolutely ethical act is not only improbable, but also structurally impossible under the regime of practical reason, precisely because reason has no access to the law of things themselves. As a result, the law speaks to man, who hears it as a nagging imperative because his will is forever divided against itself and incapable of performing a purely ethical act untainted by considerations of personal gain. What divides the will? The will is divided by the multiplicity of egos that populate the mind. This multiplicity is not accidental, but is the necessary effect of reason as the faculty of knowledge. The nature of reason is to divide and to discriminate between objects and between ego and object, but this critical activity is always positional, that is, it is carried out within a situation and from the point of view of the ego. The critical activity of reason, therefore, can never be "pure" because it can *never* be abstracted from the situation in which it takes place. On the other hand, a description of the functioning of reason at the transcendental level, like the one carried out by Kant in the *Critique*, is possible, but only by artificially separating it from its necessary errancy, which Kant calls the *pathological*. Kant concludes not only that it is impossible to determine whether an act is truly ethical judging by its appearance alone, but also that every ethical act is in fact tainted to a degree by the pathological. Thus, the ethical dimension is not a reality or even a possibility, but simply a *regulative projection of reason*. And this is why the messiah will never come, and we will never reach the kingdom of ends. However, we can turn the tables on Kant and say that since there are acts that appear to be the result of a good will, then their authentically ethical character cannot be excluded either. *Perhaps the messiah has always already come, but we have not been looking.*

It is obvious, then, that if we want to maintain the possibility of a truly ethical act, the ethical dimension cannot be founded on the faculty of reason, because to do so would be to miss the essence of ethics. We may want to ask what it is that gives the moral law the forcefulness that characterizes it. Conscience can only derive its authority from the sense of truthfulness that it inspires. But what is the origin of the feeling of truthfulness? The answer put forward by Freud is that the insistence of the moral law is due to the sense of guilt created by the internal splitting of the ego into the superego. Thus, the authority of the law rests on a negative feeling, the feeling of guilt and shame in the event of the failed accomplishment of one's duty.

What is the essence of feeling? It is perhaps necessary to return to Kant's notion of sensibility and experience. Experience is always experience of an object that is informed by sensibility, that is, by the senses, and organized and unified by reason. Just as there is no reading without a reader, there cannot be sensibility without the coordinative function of reason. It follows that there is no such thing as pure sensibility and that experience is structured from the very beginning by the categories of understanding and can take place only within those categories. The sense of certainty attached to the perception of an object in the world is the result of the harmony between sensibility and understanding. What, then, are feelings? Feelings are sensations of a more complex order because they refer not to the perception of things, but to *the perception of the relation of the ego to such perceptions*. Feelings indicate the reaction of the ego to the perception of an object, or in other words, *through feelings the ego perceives itself perceiving the object*. In this case, feelings are a function of reason as well, but in the sense of its *perversion*, because in the Kantian system neither the knowledge of the world, nor the knowledge of the supreme good require the assistance of feelings. Yet feelings are the necessary complement of the ego, just as the ego is the necessary complement of the object. But the dream of a pure reason is based on the fallacy of a knowledge achieved *without the ego*. This is why if we look into Kant's conception of ethics, we see that all the affections of the ego — feelings of pleasure or pain, happiness or sadness — are considered to be a resistance to the application of the moral law. Feelings are the *symptom* of an unwillingness to sacrifice the whole of oneself to the supreme good. They indicate the inclination to follow not the categorical, but the hypothetical imperative, the desire to pursue the relatively good — that which is good for a certain purpose — rather than the absolutely good, which results not only from obedience to the law, but from love of the law itself. *For Kant, love is always love for the moral law and as such it carries no specific feeling with it because it represents a complete identification with pure reason.* But we have already seen that the idea of a pure reason can be produced only through the foreclosure of the pathological. If we reintroduce the pathological into the system, the only evidence of the existence of the moral law is negative feelings, principally in the form of inadequacy and guilt, and with that the Freudian hypothesis of conscience as the voice of the superego is demonstrated. It is clear that Freud is a complement to Kant in that there is no "pure conscience," just as there is no "pure reason." Thus, we should mistrust our conscience just as much as we mistrust our pathological inclinations.

But is it accurate to say that the love of the law should carry no emotion with it? Perhaps it will be useful to analyze the meaning of emotion a bit further. We have seen that feelings are the result of a relative interpretation of the law aimed at the preservation of the ego. In this sense, feelings are always organized around an object. However, we have encountered a type of feeling that does not derive from a relation to an object. Let's return to what we said about the subject as that which in itself has no attributes, while being the condition for the constitution of the relation between the ego and the object. We said that the lack of predicates makes the subject *unthinkable as an object* and that Kant sees it not as a real entity but simply as a logical device necessary for the production of the transcendental ideal. We also said that the subject coincides with temporality as the infinite repetition of the present as opposed to the logical progression from the past to the future. If experience is always experience of an object, then it can take place only within the frame of time as progression, and as a consequence, the existence of the subject as temporality can never be an object of experience. That which *experiences* something, then, is *always the ego, never the subject*. But this does not authorize us to conclude, with Kant, that the subject is simply a construction of reason necessary for the production of the transcendental ideal. We must instead draw a distinction between the *mind* as the center of the faculty of reason, that which, after the dimension of the pathological has been added, psychoanalysis calls the "psyche," and the *subject* as the continuous affection of the present and of presence without which the mind — or its reverse side, the psyche — could not even begin to unfold. *The subject cannot be an object of experience because it constantly affects us as the present of our presence*. It is an affection, that is, an emotion without object that moves our will. There is no mind or psyche without a subject, and there are no feelings without pathos, without the primary affection that makes every subsequent state of mind possible, while remaining qualitatively different from them. Thus, at the very foundation of the faculty of reason we do not find the idea of totality as the transcendental substratum of reason itself, but we experience the subject as pathos, that is, as the infinite affection of presence. The limit of reason is not an anamorphosis of reason in the form of the transcendental ideal as archetype of all possible concepts. *The limit of reason is pathos and pathos is the subject of the ego and of the mind — that is, it is the subject of the faculty of reason itself.*

Let's return to the question of the essence of the moral act. Kant contends that practical reason is anchored in the intuition of the absolute good as an ideal of reason, but the absolute good can never be reached by reason because reason is a faculty of the mind and, in the final analysis, a faculty of the ego. As such, it is multiple and inescapably compromised by the pathological. In fact, we can say that *reason is constitutively perverse — reason is always impure*. On what can a truly ethical act be based then? It can be founded only on pathos, which we must carefully distinguish from the pathological, which belongs to the domain of feelings. The pathological is an effect of reason and is precisely that which covers up and prevents the recognition of the originary affection of the subject as the immediate, non-reflective *passion* of being in the duration of the now. The pathological disguises pathos as a plain ego feeling; it erases the instant in the past or the future and it enslaves the ego to its object and the object to the ego. In such conditions, a truly moral act is inconceivable. An ethical act will have to be accomplished not in relation to the idea of the absolute good, but in relation to the subject as a state of affection that allows the mind to perceive a sense of co-existence with all that is. This can happen only if the discriminating power of reason is circumvented. Without the presence of the subject as primary affectivity, any command of reason would have no compelling force and would be issued in vain. Reason is the *instrument* of the ethical impulse, not its origin.

It is the subject as pathos and as the presence of the present that provides the certainty of the existence of objects. In other words, the idea of an *omnitudo realitatis* could not invade our reason and our imagination unless it were anchored in an emotional, pre-pathological, pre-cognitive experience of continuity with all that is. Thus, if from the point of view of reason the idea of the whole is a heuristic device, from the point of view of the subject, it is immediately real, not in the form of the perception of an object, but as the affective undercurrent that underlies it and is obscured by it. While from the point of view of reason, love is the immediate and complete obedience to the law, from the point of view of the subject, love precedes and is therefore higher than the law, hence, the Christian teaching of God as love. However, the God that is love is not the same as the God of the Ten Commandments. The God of the Ten Commandments is the Kantian God, the God of reason and of duty, a God that is at once internal and external to reason without ever becoming real. But in the moment in which we become aware of the subject as the affection of the present, we also become aware that the divine is fundamentally pathos, not logos. Therefore, God is not, as Kant says, a concept that concludes and crowns the whole creation, but rather the fundamental affection, primordial and ever-present, a sound that accompanies every moment of life, at least for those who know how to listen.

How can we become aware of it? Nietzsche, for example, was able to see the difference between pathos and the pathological and made it the object of a fragment entitled "On Music and Words." Here he observes that human language is constituted by two heterogeneous elements: words and their "tonal subsoil." Words are symbols of concepts, but the tonal subsoil of language is the manifestation of sensations of pleasure or pain that accompany all other conceptions as their fundamental basis and are expressions of "*one* primal cause unfathomable to us."[17] The original sin of language is that the tonal subsoil is always captured and enslaved by the signification of words, so what seems to be an improvement in communication is in fact an impoverishment and an obfuscation of that which is communicated. Hence, the meaning and necessity of music, and secondarily, of poetry. Nietzsche writes:

> [*T*]*he Will is the object of music but not the origin of it*, that is the Will in its very greatest universality, as the most original manifestation, under which is to be understood all Becoming. That, which we call *feeling*, is with regard to this Will already permeated and saturated with conscious and unconscious conceptions and is therefore no longer directly the object of music; it is unthinkable then that these feelings should be able to create music out of themselves. Take for instance the feelings of love, fear and hope: music can no longer do anything with them in a direct way, every one of them is already so filled with conceptions. On the contrary these feelings can serve to symbolise music, as the lyric poet

does who translates for himself into the simile-world of feelings that conceptually and metaphorically unapproachable realm of the Will, the proper content and object of music. The lyric poet resembles all those hearers of music who are conscious of an *effect of music on their emotions*; the distant and removed power of music appeals, with them, to an *intermediate realm* which gives to them as it were a foretaste, a symbolic preliminary conception of music proper, it appeals to the intermediate realm of the emotions.[18]

It is not enough to be able to hear music; one must hear the music of music, and only then does one enter the realm of the Will. Most of us, however, approach it lyrically, through words, as a kind of initiatory practice, which allows the foretaste of the originary affection. It is important to point out that the will Nietzsche describes here is similar, though not exactly the same as, the notion of the subject as pathos I have tried to articulate. For Nietzsche, will has the character of activeness that is incompatible with the subject as pathos. Nietzsche's concept of the will remains captive to the opposition he set forth in *The Birth of Tragedy* between the Apollonian and the Dionysian. If the Apollonian is the dimension of language and reason, the Dionysian is conceived as its complementary opposite in the form of an anti-rationality, or irrationality, that manifests itself in ecstatic explosions of violence and frenzy. Influenced by Schopenhauer, Nietzsche fails to see that wherever there is activeness there is also purpose, signification, and reason — there cannot be a blind will, a pure will independent from reason. Reason is the essence of the will, especially when it is a Dionysian will.

In order to think the subject as pathos, we will have to come to a clearer understanding of what passivity is. The dichotomy between the Apollonian and the Dionysian is based on the *exclusion of passivity*. Each one of the two forces — in Nietzsche's conception, reason and passion — is active with respect to the other. Only when one is subjugated by the other does it become passive, and it so happens that reason always ends up ruling over its opposite, passion. The state of passivity for Nietzsche, then, is simply the forceful suppression of the natural activeness of a force. But the subject as pathos is not a force, it is not a will, it is not a drive; it is passion in the etymological sense of affection and suffering. Passivity is the mode of being of pathos as the "enabling factor" that Heidegger calls *das Vermögen*. It is a suffering without mediation and therefore without agent or object: Pathos is Being. The only way we can think the meaning of passivity is as the affection of presence that logically precedes any dualism, including that of the Dionysian and Apollonian, and not as the opposite of activity or as the resistance of the irrational to reason. A truly ethical act, then, can neither be performed on the basis of the unleashing of the Dionysian, nor founded exclusively on the judicious articulation of the transcendental ideal of the good. Practical reason can unfold only through the disclosure of the subject as pathos in its separation from the merely pathological. Paradoxically, that which is the most active — the ethical act — becomes possible and thinkable only on the ground of the instant of absolute passivity: the instant of the revelation of the subject.

1. Franz von Baader, *Sämtliche Werke* (Aalen: Scientia, 1963), 1:344. "Ich behaupte, daß, so wie man sich nicht frei bewegen kann ohne Grund zu fassen, und wie man nicht Grund fassen kann ohne freies Bewegen, man auch seine Vernuft nicht gebrauchen kann ohne frei zu glauben, und nicht glauben kann, ohne von seiner Vernuft Gebrauch zu machen" (my translation).

2. Immanuel Kant, "The End of All Things," in *Perpetual Peace and Other Essays*, trans. Ted Humphrey (Indianapolis: Hackett, 1983), 103.

3. Ibid., 102.

4. Ibid., 93.

5. Ibid.

6. Immanuel Kant, *Critique of Pure Reason*, trans. Werner S. Pluhar (Hackett: Indianapolis, 1996), 563-564.

7. See ibid., 564, note 27.

8. Ibid., 566-567.

9. Ibid., 568.

10. Kant, *Fundamental Principles of the Metaphysic of Morals*, trans. T. K. Abbott (Amherst, N.Y.: Prometheus Books, 1988), 14.

11. Ibid., 36.

12. Kant, *Critique of Pure Reason*, 616.

13. Ibid., 311.

14. Walter Benjamin, "On Perception," in *Selected Writings: 1913-1926*, ed. Marcus Bullock and Michael W. Jennings (Cambridge: Harvard University Press, 1996), 1:96.

15. Kant, *Critique of Pure Reason*, 308; emphasis added.

16. Ibid., 290.

17. Friedrich Nietzsche, "On Music and Words," in *The Complete Works of Friedrich Nietzsche* (New York: Russell & Russell, 1964), 2:31.

18. Ibid., 35.

LACK AND DESTRUCTION
alain badiou

THE SUBJECT PRECEDES ITSELF

APRIL 18, 1977

Destruction. — The more-than-real and the interruption of the repeatable. — Cure and re-education. — Two subjective allocations of force: anxiety and superego.

Destruction is a figure of the grafting (*enracinement*) of the subject in which loss not only turns lack into a cause, but also produces consistency out of excess. Through destruction, the subject attaches itself to what within lack survives, and is not the repetitive closure of the effect to the presence of the cause.

If the *structural* concept of contradiction (the splitting) implies the presence of lack and points to the horizon of the law, the *historical* concept of contradiction arises from the presence of destruction whose sphere of action lies in the *non-law*. One pole of the contradiction, which constitutes the law of the ex-place (*esplace*) as the malevolent genie of place, plays with its own absence as that which, by founding the repeatable, guarantees the perennial conservation of the world. This is the definition of a ruling class, which is never made present except where the antagonist subject is subjected to repetition. We should name such an absence "society" — for example, the French imperialist society — so as to avoid falling into the trap of subjectivation. As for the "private" subject, it is in the law of desire, and more specifically in the dyad of perversion/neurosis that we must find the reason for its flickering identity. Neurosis and perversion are the primordial subjective elements through which we enter into society with ourselves.

But the fact that the other pole of the contradiction from which the subject arises can be considered *destructive* does not allow us to reduce the subjective dialectic to neurosis, that is, to the order of socialized repetition. It is true, however, that the social is the neurosis of the political. This is what trade unionism, with its doleful and compulsive allegiance to the state and to its imperialistic repetitions, incarnates. Trade unions recognize only one lack, that of the law, and every vindication of the law is essentially "legitimate."

The political, even though it is structured in the same way, disappears in the self-imposed destruction of its very legitimacy. The destructive element cannot be inscribed on the ex-placed (*esplacé*) ground of repetition except as the excess of that which keeps it in place. This element is what we will call the *subject*. To define the subject as "the metonymy of the lack of being" only identifies half of its essence. The other half is *that which allows the lack to exist*, that is, *destruction* as that which is irreducible to the act of pure substitution.

In this way, the subject as the placed (*placé*) product of the law of lack, by following the thrust of destruction, brings out a "more-than-real" through which lack itself comes to lack. It is this "more-than-real" that I call "force." But this point needs some rectification. In the volume entitled *Theory of Contradiction* that I wrote two years ago, the notion of "force" is not really dialecticized. There force complements, or even compliments, place insofar as it is conceived as a "placed force." In this sense, it is nothing else but the quality of the process that provides the ground for the overthrowing of the place system.

I think that today it is still premature, however justified and pedagogically correct it may be, to aim at the fulfillment of the quality of the structure. It is not only because of their qualitative heterogeneity that the two terms of a contradiction turn into a relation of forces. If we remain at that level, we are reduced to a duel. The conservative term is identified with the law of lack and subordinates the other to repetition. Force is nothing but that which, being out-of-place (*hors-lieu*), concentrates in itself a term that was assigned to repetition. In this way, it jams up the mechanism of repetition and triggers the possibility for the destruction of its law. In the place where the old coherence prescribed a mere sliding, we find instead an interruption that takes place through a purification that exceeds the place. This is the history of force.

From this point of view, just as there is only *one* subject, there is also only *one* force whose existence always surfaces an event. This event, the trace of the subject, cuts across both lack and destruction. This is what happens when a revolution cuts the rising curve of the wheat price, or when death interrupts the conventions of war, or when the crowd assaults the Bastille, or when the Bolshevik political order comes into being.

The subject-support is inescapably divided between the part of itself that is subjected to repetition (as a result of being placed) and the part that interrupts and blocks repetition, thereby bringing out the non-repeatable. We are talking about something more complex than the simple distinction between force and place. These are not two concepts for the same process, but rather two processes (repetition/interruption and lack/destruction) for one concept (that of subject). Force is what separates from the repeatable and comes into being as the non-repeatable.

In order to clarify this point, it will be helpful to draw a parallel between the aim of the psychoanalytic cure and that of political re-education. Whatever the obvious and universal short-comings of either may be, it is the intention that counts...

We won't pay any attention to those who argue that a couch is not as serious as a concentra-tion camp. To them we say without hesitation that this remains to be seen. The axiom of the *nouveaux philosophes* — "a camp is a camp" — is just as false as what the Chicago therapists wanted to promote through the excommunication of Lacan: "a couch is a couch." The fact is that the psychoanalytic cure has no other real aim than that of the readjustment of the subject to its own repetition. Hence Lacan shows extreme moderation in relation to his own power as an analyst: "An analysis should not be pushed too far. When the analysand feels that he is happy to be alive, it is enough."[1]

But what does political re-education aim at? Nothing less than the overthrowing of one's subjective position, that is, the interruption of the repetitions induced by the subject's previous class identity. And in this process, happiness and "the good life" have no role to play. The psychoanalytic cure does not claim to overcome the law of lack. In fact the opposite is true: through the resolution of the symptom — which is, according to Lacan, "that which is the most real for many people"[2] — the labor of truth is directed at recreating subjection to the cause through its very oblivion. For "[e]very successful symbolic integration involves a sort of normal forgetting," and "[i]ntegration into history evidently brings with it the forgetting of an entire world of shadows which are not transposed into symbolic existence. And if this symbolic exist-ence is successful and is fully taken on by the subject, it leaves no weight behind it."[3] The aim of the psychoanalytic cure is the slightly smoother exercise of the efficacy of lack.

Political re-education, or revolutionarization, entirely deserves the charge made against it of "wanting to change people," "brainwashing," "destroying individuality," or, as Mao says, of wanting to "change man in his innermost being." This is the avowed end of the cultural revolu-tion; it presupposes the conviction that the old man can die. Look at the reverse side of these accusations: they are nothing but a plea for the eternal oblivion of the loss that constitutes the I. They are a mere defense of the right to repetition. The paradox of this line of defense is evident. When asked about what should be expected from an analysis, Lacan answers that one should expect to be rid of one's symptom. "A symptom is curable," he says.[4] But what is a symptom? "The so-called neurotic symptom is simply something that allows them to keep on living."[5] Should we be delivered from what is most real for us, from that which allows us go on living? To live with one's own truth causes a symptom because that which should be absent is instead in excess.

For this reason the cure doesn't really aim at an attunement of the All to the true. Too rigorous a pursuit of the true would lead to psychosis: "Thank God, we don't make them (the analysands) so normal that they will end up psychotic. That's the point where we must be very cautious."[6] The point is rather to deliver the real to the oblivion of its oblivion, where causal force will be purified in the lack, and we will have an attunement of the true to the All. This type of work requires moderation.

But the process of revolutionarization does not call for history; in fact it cheats it — it cuts the true into pieces in the very integrity of its *schize*. It is the ambition to turn the old order into a symptom and to produce a *crisis* by showing the total truth of the symptom. This is what takes us into the domain of ethics, and of the strictest kind of ethics at that. Is it at all possible to make sense of resistance if the identity of the subject derives from the repeatable and from the law of lack? And is it possible to appraise the value of destruction from which both the possibility of the mastery of loss and the opening of a space for the new derive?

The analytic cure, revolutionarization...As usual, facts in themselves give us no evidence in either direction. Between the veterans of the couch and the militants of groups like the *Gauche Proletarienne*, we really cannot say that the debate in the seventies has brought much that is valuable. Let's try first to maintain the disjunction between the two subjective moments — for its articulation is hard — and then to graft onto it the moment of a founding destruction that is also the bliss of its possible failure.

If Lacan is a dialectician, he should be able to realize what he doesn't. That is to say that he will rejoin Hegel only on the condition of being able to take the structural primacy of the law of lack to its other extreme, where it turns into destruction and the more-than-real of force. "Force," however, is a term that he dislikes intensely, busy as he is fighting the pride of the American economists. "Psychic energy," quantity, flow: all this is *ignorantiae asylum*. He proceeds from epistemological mistrust (and he doesn't mince his words): "How often, in the course of history, have the notions of energy and force been taken up and used again upon an increasingly total-ized reality!"[7] — to the significant verdict — "force is used to designate a locus of opacity."[8] We won't find any satisfaction here. I propose that there are two themes in Lacan that indicate what happens to the more-than-real of destruction and to the breach of the algebra of the subject, both on the side of lack and on that of the mark. These two themes are anxiety and the superego.

The principal reference when it comes to the superego is as follows:

> The super-ego has a relation to the law, and is at the same time a senseless law, going so far as to become a failure to recognise [*méconnaissance*] the law. That is always the way we see the super-ego acting in the neurotic. Isn't it because the morality of the neurotic is a senseless, destructive, purely oppressive, almost always anti-legal morality, that it became necessary to elaborate on the function of the super-ego in analysis?

> The super-ego is at one and the same time the law and its destruction. As such, it is speech itself, the commandment of law, in so far as nothing more than its root remains. The law is entirely reduced to something, which cannot even be expressed, like the *You must*, which is speech deprived of all its meaning. It is in this sense that the super-ego ends up by being identified with only what is most devastating, most fascinating, in the primitive experiences of the subject. It ends up being identified with what I call *the ferocious figure*, with the figures which we can link to primitive traumas the child suffered, whatever these are.[9]

The superego gives access to the source of the force of law, to that which is no longer of the order of language but which lies at the core of the imperative character of the law. If the law can resist destruction — the excess of the repetition that the law itself articulates — it is because the very order of the law, which takes the form of an imperative, is in itself excess and destruction.

This is the first sign of what I will describe as the eternal precedence of the subject to itself. The law shows that the subject must sustain itself and at the same time break out of itself in order to accomplish the splitting that defines it. In this sense, Lacan says that the superego functions as an opening, however sinister. The non-law is what manifests itself as the affirmative of the law; for this reason the superego can be simultaneously the sign of the law and of its destruction. The superego originates where there is an out-of-place (*hors-place*) of the imperative concerning every place, that is, where there is a non-repetition of the prescription to repeat. It is precisely there that the paralyzing (and therefore destructive) function of the superego becomes manifest, as is shown in the absurdity of obsessional neurosis and, in the case of the political subject, in the comfort taken in the presence of the state. In neurosis and the realm of irrational legislation, the superego sustains a destructive morality, a naked imperative, that forces every symbolic articulation into a syncope. Let's put aside for now the fact that so far all of this has been described negatively (absurdity, and so on). What counts is that an interruption as such takes place.

As for anxiety, it is from the point of view of the real in excess rather than from that of the law of lack that it functions as interruption — and therefore as revelation. "[A]nxiety is a crucial term of reference, because in effect anxiety is that which does not deceive. But anxiety may be lacking. In experience, it is necessary to canalize it and, if I may say so, to take it in small doses, so that one is not overcome by it. This is a difficulty similar to that of bringing the subject into contact with the real — a term that I shall try to define next time."[10] Anxiety is the result of the submersion by the real, of the radical excess of the real over the lack. It is the destruction of the symbolic network by what reveals itself, here in the opening, of the unspeakable encounter. It is necessary to channel anxiety's effect, since it destroys the adjustment to the repeatable. It short-circuits the lamp of the subject to the real. Anxiety, then, is the sign of that which in the subject forces the legal ex-place. As Lacan says beautifully, anxiety is nothing but the lack of lack. But when the lack comes to lack, its metonymic effect is interrupted and a mastery of real loss has to start, which is paid for with the ravaging of all symbolic points of reference. Hence anxiety never lies. Destruction must meet the law of lack in order to sweep away deception, the semblant, and the oblivion of oblivion.

Anxiety and the superego are therefore two fundamental concepts of the subject (although there are another two), two designations of that which lies at the crossing of the inert and civilized law of lack and the barbaric interruption of destruction. These two concepts have been recognized by Lacan, one in the paralyzing horror of obsession, the other in the ravaging truth of the plunge into the real. Although they weren't in tune with his theoretical line, he nonetheless acknowledged them because of the rigorousness of his experiment. As the accomplished dialectician that he indeed was...

TORSION   MAY 2, 1977

A dialectical use of the mathematical text. — Torsion. — Subjective formulas. — First notes on justice and courage.

I would like to talk about a certain use of mathematics that is my own and doesn't belong to anyone else, neither the mathematicians, who find it metaphorical, nor others, who are intimidated by it. The point is to short-circuit dialectical analysis by the examination of the way in which mathematics treats a word so that both rigorousness and its interpretive value are maintained. It is indeed a question of interpretation, or rather of representation in the theatrical sense of the term.

The postulate is that no signifier finds a place in a mathematical text randomly, and if it is true that its mathematical character derives from its function within the structure of the demonstration, it is also true that this structure should be considered, in its overdetermination, as the retroactive analysis of its very non-random character. This means that we consider the mathematical signifier a symptom around which the deductive text attempts an auto-analysis. That is, we envision the mathematical text as the analyst of some of its own signifiers as being symptomatic of itself. We will have to compare this type of analysis with others deriving from different theories, such as the dialectical and materialistic theory of the subject, in order to gauge the result of the speculation. All this is based on the assumption that when formalism's mathematical position encounters language, a desubjectivation takes place that eradicates the signifiers that suture the subject. Consider the fascination that Marx and Engels had for differential calculus and their desire to find in it the matrix of the "dialectical law"; or the fallacy of Marx's conviction — testified to by his numerous writings on mathematics — that he was a mathematician because he was a dialectician. The enigmatic quality of these writings is tied to the phantasm of a formalized dialectic, of which mathematics is a specialized application, but also the privileged terrain that displays its universal principle.

We must avoid falling into this temptation and take notice of the fact that, as I will show you, words resonate within a demonstration well beyond pure inference, even though their echo is audible only in the moment of the actual understanding of the chain of explanation. I'll give you an example. We have already seen that the term "torsion" designates the subject-point of convergence of the other three classic determinations of truth: the All, coherence, and repetition. It has occurred to me that, besides its topological use (as in the torsion of a knot, Lacan's employment of the term), the word "torsion" is used also in algebra in a very simple way. Let's posit a group, which, I remind you, is a set defined by a law of composition among its elements that I will mark "+," and which has the canonical properties of being associative $(x + (y + z)) = ((x + y) + z)$; of having a neutral element, "0," such that $(x + 0) = x$; and of associating each element with its inverse (that is, $- x$, with $(x + (- x)) = 0$). We call the "torsion" of an element x of a group the smallest whole number n, if it exists, such that if x is added to itself n times, it will equal zero:

$$x + x + x + \ldots + x = 0$$
$$\underbrace{}$$
$$\text{n times}$$

For the purposes of notation, let's call the following series "nx":

$$x + x + \ldots + x$$
$$\underbrace{}$$
$$\text{n times}$$

An element that has a torsion is a torsion element, a contorted element. A group in which every element has a torsion is a torsion group. For every element x of this group, there is a whole number n such that $nx = 0$. This "torsion" is not my invention. It's been in mathematics for at least fifty years. (Unfortunately, I have not looked into the history of this signifier.)

Observe the way mathematicians analyze the choice of this word, that is, in what way the mathematical chain represents a "torsion":

1) Let's examine the definition. It is evident that torsion is connected to repetition, that is, the repetition of the operation of the group applied n times to the same element. We could say that the element *insists* in the addition $x + x + x + \ldots + x + \ldots$ because it is *serialized*. Every

partial addition is particular, but when there is torsion — that is, when the designated number of repetitions is reached — the sum is zero. In this sense, we will say that *torsion interrupts repetition*, which is the reason for its dialectical status.

Torsion interrupts repetition in the qualitative character of the different additions. If torsion were surpassed, we would find once again the previous partial sums. If $nx = 0$, we will have $nx + x = 0 + x = x$, and $nx + 2x = x + x$, and finally $nx + nx = 0 + 0 = 0$.

In this case, the partial additions return, being an "excess of zero" that surpasses the preceding terms before torsion brings us back to zero. This means that algebraic torsion wipes away all the past additions where the element insists.

2) Is it necessary to conclude that torsion modifies the ordinary laws of a group? It is to be expected that since it does so by discovering a new type of coherence, torsion does not overlap with the various repetitive series that make up the fabric of the All. This is its crucial function as an interruption. In Marxist terms, it is the paradoxical status of the party. In mathematics, this point is analyzed through a very simple theorem that states that the axiomatic theory of torsion groups is not presentable in a first-degree logic.

A first-degree logic is one in which quantifiers ("it exists," $\exists$, and "for all," $\forall$) are only applied to individual variables. In this type of logic, for example, you can write: "there is an element having the property P," or alternatively: $\exists x(P(x))$. But you cannot write: "there is a property p having a characteristic A." First-degree logic is generally sufficient for normal purposes, although it employs an infinite number of axioms for each single theory.

There is a case that particularly interests us, however, precisely because it does not involve torsion. It is the case of groups in which no element different from zero is submitted to torsion. These are called *torsion-free groups*, groups with absolutely no torsion that are, in other words, completely "straight." This case of "straightness" troubles the dialectician. In these groups, x is added to itself without ever interrupting the process of repetition. Now, the theory of torsion-free groups, that is, the theory of algebraic straightness, is easily presentable in a first-degree logic. Take the infinite list of axioms that say that for every element x different from 0, the repetition of additions of itself will never amount to zero:

Ax. 1: $(\forall x)\ (x + x \neq 0)$

Ax. 2: $(\forall x)\ (x + x + x \neq 0)$ Taking as the domain of the quantifier

....   all x different from 0.

Ax. $(n - 1)$: $(\forall x)\ (nx \neq 0)$

....

If we add this to the three fundamental axioms of groups, we have the theory of the first order of torsion-free groups. Why? Because you cannot know for each number what whole number represents its torsion; you only know that it exists. Thus, it should be possible to write: "for every element x, there is at least one whole number n such that nx = 0," or: $(\forall x)\,(\exists n)\,(nx = 0)$.

$(\exists n)$ applies the quantifier *not* to an individual variable, but to the property "whole number," that is, to a predicate. In this way, we exceed first-degree logic. Therefore, the logic of the theory of torsion is qualitatively more complex than that of the theory of straightness.

As a consequence the dialectician has resolved his problem. In fact, he will happily find that the existential uncertainty that looms over the effectiveness of torsion hinders the functioning of first-degree logic. If the axioms of algebraic straightness are insufficient, it is because they are all universal and determined by $\forall$, that is, by the "for all" whose logical simplicity and masculine character we know very well. A theory in which the axioms are all universal has a set of consistent properties. In particular, every substructure of a model of this theory is itself a model of such a theory.

However, the existential that marks the limit of the theory of torsion exceeds the logical plane that sustains the universal, and appears as the figure of the unknown quantity within all repetition and as the indeterminate within all rupture. In this case, mathematics justifies the *tabula rasa* of successful revolutions.

3) Torsion groups that are infinite — although all finite groups are also torsion groups, the finite does not interest us here — can, in spite of everything, have consistent algebraic properties if they are commutative. A group is commutative if regardless of the value of x and y, we have: x + y = y + x.

In this case, the conclusions are:

—The elements that have the same torsion n form a subgroup.

—The group is made up of the direct product of the subgroups, and each of these subgroups is composed of elements whose torsion is p^q, where p is a whole number.

I don't want to take up too much time explaining these statements. What they say is that in a universe of communication and reversibility, torsions determine a set of regulated subgroups and divide the initial group into substructures whose identity principle is clear.

The subversive value of torsion is toned down into an analytical law, into a conceptual vector that allows for a reasonable partitioning of the All. In other words, torsion tends towards the segmentation of the All into local coherences in which repetition is minimal. It is as if from the point of view of a reversible historical space, revolutions had no other function than to serialize events, to classify the epochs and to reconnect and re-group the heterogeneous. Or as if the party — when it conflates with the state, for example — had no other function than to bring out the repetitive segmentation of history through that spectacular element of commutation that we call the "restoration of capitalism."

But in the final analysis, history is not commutative. This would be the very principle of its inexistence, within which lies the law of torsion. What, then, does the algebraist tell us about non-commutative infinite torsion groups? Well, not much. He leaves it to us.

4) The only hope is that a non-commutative torsion group generated by a finite number of elements will be in itself finite. Why is this an anti-dialectical hope? Because in this way we would have connected the values of two finitudes: the finitude of torsion that blocks the infinity of the repeatable, and the finitude that engenders the group and controls the twisted (*tordue*) dialectic that puts torsion's finite unknown quantity to work in the non-commutative infinity of the group.

A finite-generated group is one whose elements can be presented as the sums (with possible repetitions) of elements taken from a finite stock. If, for example, we have a stock of three elements — a, b, c — every element of the group will appear as (a + a), (a + b + a + c), (c + b + a) — and these are only arbitrary examples. Obviously two combinations can be the same (that is, they can yield the same element). Thus a finite-generated group is not necessarily infinite.

Since in a torsion group all repetition of the addition of an element to itself is interrupted (that is, returns to zero), and since this is true in particular for the elements of the finite stock that generate the set, one can have the impression that it is not possible to have an infinity of different combinations of additions. Intuitively, one can see that there is the chance that a finite-generated torsion group is itself finite. From a dialectical point of view, this would constitute a problem.

Marxism's field of operation has three analogical properties: it is infinite, it has torsion, and it is finite-generated. Why? First, because the event-element (*l'élément événementiel*), which is the raw material of mass politics, is infinite. It is infinite at every moment because its theoretically-countable nature, from a political point of view, is simply fictional. Second, because repetition is interrupted by the event in order to produce in the All a different coherence of the torsion point. And finally, because the presentation elements of all politics — classes — are definitely a finite number.

A deductive analysis of the term "torsion" from an algebraic point of view would show a divergence, a sort of exploratory hazard, if the finite-generated torsion group were finite. From a dialectical point of view, in this case, the mathematical interpretation of the term would be in a position of control over the excess. But this is not the case because the theorem of Shafarevitch shows that it is not true that all finite-generated torsion groups are finite. It demonstrates this by way of a counterexample, through a group generated by three torsion elements that is nonetheless infinite. The existence of such a group brings the analysis of the term "torsion" back into the domain of dialectics. As a result, infinite and non-commutative torsion groups have only exceptional properties. As algebra shows, they are at the limit of the algebraic unnameable.

Torsion is the limit of algebra. Torsion is perverse — it is a subject. Note that we haven't presented a model here, nor have we attempted to "mathematicize" anything. We have only tried to bring out a sort of surplus brilliance whose only means of expression remains the mathematical text insofar as it is the objective elucidation of the symptom. What happens, however, when the deductive analysis of the mathematical signifier that we have isolated diverges from its dialectical interpretation? In this case, we will have the audacity to say that a new mathematical hypothesis must resolve the divergence. We maintain that no term comes into use by chance. This will be a way, however unorthodox, to incite the present mathematical theory to formulate a new theorem. Mathematics is the science of the real, and its signifiers may be many, but they are still countable.

What algebraic notation will we have to use, then, to indicate the superego and anxiety? Consider that these two concepts designate neither a subjective experience, nor a part of the subject, but rather two processes whose combination defines that region of practical materiality that we should call the "subject-effect." No subject pre-exists anxiety or remains beyond the superego if subjective anxiety and the superego are the modes of consistency of the subject-effect. Here we construct the concept of the subject starting from much more general dialectical categories: force (F), space (S), truth (T), place (P), destruction (d), and lack (l).

Anxiety is the excess-of-the-real (*trop de réel*) (force) over what can be symbolized in a certain order (space). From this order the subject emerges already divided, crushed from its birth by its own truth — a truth that abides by the law of lack and, as a result, itself comes to lack. Thus, if ∟ indicates the excess, then this is the figure for anxiety:

$$F \diagup S = \frac{T + 1 \, (l)}{\$}$$

The sign "=" indicates that it is in terms of excess, within the differential form of subjectivation, that the subject exists as split.

As far as the superego is concerned, if we name the aspect of the non-law that adheres destructively to the law itself, and if we posit that L = law (or the place [*lieu*], or the ex-place), we will have:

$$F \diagup S \longrightarrow \frac{L + d}{\$}$$

Here "⟶" means that it is within the order of the full and non-differential effect of consistency (of the subjective process) that the subject maintains itself in effacement, while being all along submitted to the intrinsic ferocity of the law's terrorizing interpellation. As you can see, this is the question of Oedipus and of Sophocles. To say that anxiety shows the way to truth means that it is in the form of a non-placed (*implaceé*) force — and not in the logic of places — that a sufficient quantity of subject-effect splits off and produces a new knowledge. This is the enunciation of torsion (it is only through it that the other three names of truth — coherence, the All, and repetition — are generated) that Mao, at the peak of the Cultural Revolution, re-translated as "troubles are an excellent thing." An excellent thing, that is, if we want to see clearly.

The definition of anxiety, then, is the trouble of seeing clearly. This is at the same time the definition of courage, but in order to see this we have to find our way through the schism presented in Greek tragedy. It is certainly true that truth in the register of anxiety is unlivable because of its essential link to lack, and it is Mallarmé who has elucidated its latent structure. It is unlivable to the extent that — constituting an interruption of the efficacy of the symbolic, a sort of hole — it is never reducible to the totality of the said. Being only half-said (*midite*), the truth is cursed (*maux-dite*). This is why truth — that of Oedipus, and of Sophocles, the truth that demands the violent sacrifice of the gaze — is an effect of the tragic.

There is, however, another truth and another tragedy: that of Orestes and of Aeschylus. There, destruction makes possible a subject who knows how to master loss. No longer T/$, but S/T̶. What does this mean if not that in this way we come out of the radical impasse in which the unity of the place and the insurmountable fixity of the symbolic has forced us? Destruction becomes dialectically linked to loss in the non-representable supposition (a supposition that is almost ineffable itself, even though it is the foundation of the univocity [*uni-dire*] of the truth) that the ex-place is divisible. The subject as the overgrowth (*transcroissance*) of the revolt of anxiety is born out of the violent internal rupture of the law, and is the process through which the order that the subject sustains in its truth is constituted as other than the subject.

Neither the other of Lacan, nor the Other can conceive of this type of alterity, which is the only one that allows us to think the advent of revolutions, the only one that allows us to understand in what sense, as Marx says, the communist revolution breaks most radically with all traditional ideas. This type of alterity is also the only one that can name the heteronomy of the political. Within this divided law and this broken symbolic, we deal with a trans-Other (*trans-Autre*) that lies at the origin of the groundwork for the determination of the other and the same.

In this sense, we must say that, historically, we witness the advent of a subject at the intersection of lack and destruction, and at the point of anxiety, but in the inversion of its truth. And this subject derives from something the existence of which Lacan denies — an other of the Other where that which stands for the first Other is no longer a disguised modality of the Same.

This is precisely what Athena does at the end of Aeschylus' *Oresteia* when, in order to interrupt the family vendetta, she appoints a tribunal such that the new laws would overthrow the old ones. The courage of the schism of the laws, the anxiety of an opaque persecution, the superego of the blood-thirsty Erinyes, and finally justice according to the consistency of the new — four concepts to articulate the subject.

In 1954, Lacan implicitly indicated the necessity of these four concepts when he started to put forth the ethical reach of his discipline:

> Once the number of cycles necessary for the subject's objects to appear have been accomplished, and his imaginary history is completed, once the successive tensed-up, suspended, anxiety-provoking desires of the subject are named and reintegrated, all is not, for all that, brought to term. What was initially there, in O, then here in O', then again in O, has to be referred to the completed system of symbols. The very outcome of the analysis requires it.

> Where could this adjournment come to a stop? Do we have to extend analytic intervention to the point of becoming one of those fundamental dialogues on justice and courage, in the great dialectical tradition?

> That is a question. It is not easy to answer, because in truth, modern man has become singularly unused to broaching these grand themes. He prefers to resolve things in terms of conduct, of adaptation, of group morale and other twaddle.[11]

Anxiety does not lie and the superego turns destruction into the consistency of the legal order. But the "fundamental dialogues on justice and courage" open the way to that aspect of the dialectical tradition in which, by virtue of a completely different grasp on the irruption of the real, the subject as *force* can force the excess over the place.

THE THEORY OF THE SUBJECT: SOPHOCLES/AESCHYLUS   MAY 9, 1977

Justice and the superego: non-law as law and law as non-law. — Joseph Conrad. — Courage and Anxiety. — Sophocles according to Hölderlin. — The decree of Athena in Aeschylus. — Reversal of the native place and reversal of exile.

"[O]nce the successive tensed-up, suspended, anxiety-provoking desires of the subject are named and reintegrated,"[12] psychoanalysis operates as a reduction of the excess-of-the-real; it reintegrates within an ex-place of symbolization what in the place kept the subject at the mercy of anxiety. Thus, force is put back in its place. But, as Lacan says, this doesn't mean that everything has been resolved. How is this so? The question is important because the dialectical extension of the theory of the subject depends on it. In other words, what is at stake here is the recognition, on the solid ground of structural effects, of their excessive reverse side through which history returns as subjective novelty. The excess-of-the-real, then, detached from its obscure readability in the truth of anxiety, must be able to stretch the symbolic order and not simply to replace what functions as the out-of-place (*horlieu*).

Here Lacan offers a grandiose perspective: "it is in as much as the subjective drama is integrated into a myth which has an extended, almost universal human value, that the subject brings himself into being."[13] Consequently, there seems to be an extensive and universalizing productivity of the "subjective drama" that the psychoanalytic work can decode by means of the "fundamental dialogues on justice and courage." Why justice and courage? Justice is the function of the subject's tie to the place, that is, to the law, and represents the divisible figure of its transformation, whereas the superego is the representation of the ferocious archaism of the fixity of the law. Justice makes no sense as a constitutive category of the subject if the symbolic operates on indivisibility and founds the subject on terror and obsessive repetition. It requires a dialectical precariousness of the law that is shaken and finally ruptured. This is not the precariousness of a particular law, but of the very imperative character of the law. More radically, from the point of view of the constitution of the subject-effect, justice is the possibility that the non-law might function as law.

This fact is well known to Marxists. The effect of the superego is that the essential and constitutive core of the state — class domination — is always dictatorial. Under the pretense of defending the law and parliamentary democracy, the state is the quintessential illegal agent of all legality, of the violence of right, and of the law as non-law. On the other hand, the communist project is justice, the claim that the non-law can become the last law of proletarian politics. Communism, the only modern theory of revolution, realizes the type of subjectivity that can sustain the universal principle of justice, that is, the non-law as law. For this reason, what is extended (the "extended, almost universal" value of Lacan) must grow out of what is in excess (of the place, of location, of the symbolic, and of the law).

Poetry gives us an example of this by way of the fragmentation of ordinary prose that extends the limit of the communicable and causes an opening of the inaccessible frontiers of the mother tongue (*lalangue*). It is not by chance that Joseph Conrad, the writer of anxiety and the super-ego — as *Heart of Darkness* and *Lord Jim* testify — gave art the strategic task of "rendering the highest kind of justice in the visible universe."[14] For this reason, he also became the writer of courage: see *The Rover* for men and *The Arrow of Gold* for women.

Courage is the non-subjection to the symbolic order at the urging of the dissolutive injunction of the real. Arising in response to the excess-of-the-real, courage is identical to anxiety, but as a disruptive force within the ex-place, it functions as its inversion. Through the disruption of communication, courage brings disorder into the symbolic, whereas anxiety is simply an invocation of death. Since courage is not an attribute of the subject, but rather the divisible process of its intrinsic existence, it is more appropriate to compare it to *fortitudo* (fortitude or strength of mind) than to *audacia* (audacity) because the opposite of courage is not fear, but anxiety. See Spinoza's *Ethics* on this (Part III, beginning with theorem 59). *Audacia* is entirely defined by the mediation of the Other; it is "the desire whereby any one is incited to do anything with a danger which his equals dare not encounter."[15] *Fortitudo*, rather, is intrinsic because it refers to the true, S/T, where by the true we mean "[a]ll actions which follow from the emotions which have reference to the mind, in so far as it is active or understands."[16] The true is the result of a deficiency in the symbolic produced by the thrust of the real. From this deficiency the subject derives its force, which is proportional to the measure of its courage in the face of the radical absence of any security. In this situation, the subject loses its name; as one of Spinoza's theorems says, security desubjectifies. What he means is that security is not a virtue, but rather is the sign of subjective impotence.

Anxiety results from the deficiency of the place, while courage is the assumption of the real by which the place is disrupted. Anxiety and courage share the same causality in a reversible articulation of the point reached by loss. On the necessary basis of anxiety and of the superego, courage and justice also articulate the subject-effect as the division of the symbolic order by the excess, that is, as the ex-place where such an excess is in-placed (*s'implace*). Hence a political subject comes into being only by giving rebellion a revolutionary value, by tying destruction to reconstruction. It will become apparent in the real that every order and every legal injunction, however stable they may seem, end up internally dividing themselves. The Other must let itself be divided into an unknown Other that it never was, and into a Same whose identity it had never prescribed.

There is a theory of the subject according to Sophocles and one according to Aeschylus. The latter (which is historically the first, but is still the second for Freud) entirely dialecticizes its other because, besides anxiety and the superego whose identities it retains, it postulates that courage and justice are the necessary operators of the subject-effect. It goes without saying that Sophocles and Aeschylus are signifiers — that is, they are concepts, not names or literary works. They are texts, but meant for the theater, which makes all the difference.

The limit of the psychoanalytic contribution to the theory of the subject can be evaluated by asking the following question: why is its theory of the subject essentially based on Sophocles, that is, predicated on the Oedipus complex? I propose instead that we refer to Aeschylus. Lacan sides with Sophocles, but aims at Aeschylus, which is where we want to get. Hölderlin opens the debate in his "Remarks on 'Antigone,'" where he describes Sophocles in the following way:

1) The type of contradiction dealt with by Greek tragedy is that of the originary versus the formal, of what is native versus what is learned (according to Hölderlin, the "natively Greek" is opposed to the "native form"). This is a division of the native place, an internal contradiction that opposes the simple foundation of the law to the law itself. In terms of ex-place, tragedy is the *parousia* of an internal division that separates the One of the ex-place from its function, which is that of regulating the multiple. Tragedy is an avatar of the contradiction between the One and the All that produces the subject.

2) For the Greeks, this contradiction sets in opposition: first, from the point of view of the originary One, its infinite and orgiastic, "Asiatic" consistency; and second, from the point of view of the regulated (civilized) ex-place that is the origin of this One, its power of representative closure that can be found in the formal perfection of Greek art, mathematics, architecture, and politics.

Let's reformulate this: if the Greek law is finitude and closure, the non-law that is the foundation of this law is the plasticity of Asia. Thus, the law as non-law, the realization of the Greek superego as consistency of the subject, is *elucidated* in tragedy.

3) In Sophocles' *Antigone,* the contradiction that informs and elucidates the tragedy is set in motion by insurrection. The fratricidal rebel turns against the city and as a result, is radically excluded by it (he is killed and his body is left unburied). But the attempt at exclusion fails: the polis enters a crisis, not as a result of a political insurrection, but as a result of the infinite absence of a limit within the native form.

4) This infinite absence of a limit produces a reversal — it is a subjectivation thanks to which the place reveals the contradictory origin and unlawful unity under the inflated framework of regulations.

5) This reversal takes on the theatrical figure of an antagonism:

—The infinite absence of a limit within the native form results in an excess-of-form (Creon). The law is revealed as being in excess of its own restorative function. Creon is the super-law.

—In reaction to this excess of form, the formless is set ablaze through the invocation of the infinite of the sky against the finite law of the polis (Antigone).

"Creon" is the name of the superego: the deregulated law — destroyed and, by its very own essence, returned as an excess of the space that it circumscribes. "Antigone" is the name of anxiety, that is, the principle of the infinity of the real that insists in the regulated finitude of the place. From this point of view, Antigone and Creon, although antagonists in the play, contribute to the same process, the formation of the Sophoclean tragic subject. Such is the foundation of this tragedy as One-text (*texte-Un*): to present the subject-process through the articulation of anxiety and the superego.

We will formulate the problem by isolating Hölderlin's two major theses:

—The effect (the dynamics) of insurrection is that of a reversal by which the advent of the new is barred.

—The internal engine of the tragic is that of the excess of the law over itself, the figure of Creon. The formless is set on fire only as a reaction at a later stage. As for the figure of the rebel, it has no room for action; it is simply an algebraic term, an absent cause subtracted from the polis. Those that turn against one another are the excess of form and the formless, the superego and anxiety — intertwined figures of the primordial One, the One of the reversal.

Thus, we ask: what is the link between these two theses? What is the politics underlying Hölderlin's poetics? The possible modernity of the tragic, like the question of the theory of the subject, is a political question.

For Hölderlin, contradiction is tragic because it leaves no way out other than death. Why? Because there is no new right that can articulate it. In the two terms (Creon and Antigone), it is the infinite form that pervades everything, that is, the real that submerges the symbolic and the native force that dissolves the place. The unity of opposites prevails over their division to the extent that the essence of the process lies in the already-there of the origin. Hence the Sophoclean name of every subject-process is reversal. Oedipus, in the clarity of his blindness, incarnates this idea. And I believe this subjective figure, whose dialectic is built on anxiety and the superego, always prevails in times of decadence and disarray, both in history and in life. For this reason, it is necessary to articulate the difference between Aeschylus and Sophocles.

In Aeschylus' *Oresteia*, the tragic is set in motion by the murder of Agamemnon. Orestes is forced to kill his mother (who has in turn killed his father) by the intricate logic of revenge and counter-revenge. This space of repetition is one in which a murder is punished by another murder. Here the unlimited is the debt of blood. The (future) Sophoclean categories are clearly present — they are connected to the ex-place itself, the palace where Orestes takes refuge after the murder that subjectivizes him through anxiety and where he is pursued by the pack of the Erinyes (the watchdogs of the superego and cruel custodians of the repetition that sets off the family vendetta).

But the true orientation of the trilogy is the rupture that allows for the advent of the new. What is at stake is the interruption of the infinite debt, of the repetitive chain of murders, by way of a torsion imposed by the ex-centered intervention of Athena. It is the advent of a new right that can completely reconfigure the logic of decision. Thanks to the tribunal set in place by Athena, the repetition of the series that made up the previous order is interrupted and a new coherence is instituted. All of a sudden the two antagonistic positions are no longer articulated by the unity of the native as in Sophocles/Hölderlin. Instead they are the internal division of that which constitutes them, a division beyond the law of what can have a legal value. It is the location (*lieu*) that is shown to be in essence not one, but two. In the course of this dialectical process, the new prevails over the old. In Hölderlin's language, we could call this, not the reversal, but the advent of the native form.

These two positions are made explicit in the trilogy. We can see the first one in the chorus of the Erinyes:

> Catastrophe now is coming from new ordinances, if a justice which is harm to justice shall prevail for this man here, the matricide. This day's work will at once accustom all men to licence...Justice's house falls. There is a place where terror is good, and a watch on minds by fear seated above. It is well to learn wisdom through grief. Would any that nurses no terror in his heart's clear light — both man and city the same — revere Justice still?...the man who defies out of boldness, transgressing [while he carries] his great cargo, one randomly got without right, in violence, will lower sail with time, once trouble catches him up and his yard-arm shatters. He calls on those who do not hear, from the whirlpool's centre so hard to struggle with; and god laughs over a hot-headed man, when he sees one who was confident that he would never be caught impotent in helpless torment, and not surmounting the wave-top. His prosperity, life-long till then, is dashed upon Justice's reef; he dies unwept, unseen.[17]

Thus, the dialectic between anxiety and the superego is the only foundation of measurement in the chain of revenge. Justice is subordinated to the superego and the structural regularity of punishment. As a result, subjectivation occurs through anxiety and under the sign of death.

The second position is enunciated by Athena, the founder of the new right:

> *Athena*: Now hear my ordinance, people of Athens, who are judging the pleas in the first trial for shed blood. For the future too this council of jurors shall always exist for Aegeus' people...Untouched by desires for gain, revered, quick to anger, the land's wakeful guardian of those asleep, this council I now establish. This has been my lengthy exhortation to my citizens for the future; and you must rise and take your votes for casting and decide the case with respect for your oath. My speech is said...And Orestes wins even if in the judgement he has equal votes. Empty the votes from the urns at once, you jurors who have this duty put on you!...

> *Apollo*: Count the emptied votes correctly, strangers, with reverent care against a wrong determination! When good judgement's gone away, great harm happens; but if a single vote comes in, it can set a house upright.

> *Athena*: The man here goes free on the charge of bloodshed. The numbers of votes are equal.[18]

Thus, because the old right lacks a limit, a new right must be instituted that puts an end to the vendetta. This requires the divisible courage of the Council, which intrinsically refers to the justice of number. The fact that everyone is given an equal right to speak signifies a radical change in the understanding of what it means to make a decision. It is a division in the very essence of right. Athena's decree produces an egalitarian torsion that sets up a new juridical coherence — the deliberation of the majority without appeal that, once applied and practiced, interrupts the mechanical repetition of revenge.

There are, then, two categories of the tragic in Greek drama: the tragic according to Aeschylus, predicated on the advent of justice out of contradiction and through the courage of the new; and the tragic according to Sophocles, based on the anxiety caused by the quest, through reversal, for the superegoic origin.

What does Hölderlin say? "The true language of Sophocles, since Aeschylus and Euripides know more how to depict suffering and wrath, yet less how to depict man's understanding as wandering below the unthinkable."[19] Here I object to the fact that, first of all, it is not possible to pair Aeschylus with Euripides. But this is only the sign of a much deeper distortion: a partially unexplained predilection for Sophocles. This is also present in Freud — who can deny that the native logic of the unconscious is by no means exempt from the reversal?

However, Aeschylus' contribution consists of the capacity to grasp, on the ground of the superego, the moment of the *institutive disruption*. There is never a return to order in his theater, but rather the constitution of a different order. Aeschylus excludes the presupposition of a unity of the originary. For this reason, the Aeschylean man does not march on the side of the unthinkable. Aeschylus is on the side of the thinkable. His virtue lies in the ability to deflect the reversal, or rather the ability to expose a non-native reversal. In this way, it is no longer the formal excess that prevails, but rather the refusal in the sign of courage. Although devoured by anxiety, and in fact *precisely because of it*, Orestes does not internalize the law of the debt of blood, nor does he turn against it in a blind fury. Instead, he demands a discussion based on facts; he resists and does not give in to the murderous seduction of the Erinyes. "Orestes" is first the name of anxiety and then of courage. "Athena" is the name of justice.

Antigone, Creon, Orestes, and Athena name the whole range of subject-effects within Greek tragedy: the formless, the formal excess, interruption, and reconstitution. In a tragedy by Aeschylus, the dynamics of insurrection, as Hölderlin would say, do not coincide with the propagation of death. Aeschylus is the founder of justice through internal division and the decline of the old right. Far from being suspended in the exclusion of the absent cause, the rebel — Orestes or Prometheus — is the agent of this dynamics. Hölderlin clearly opts for the Sophoclean tragic, that is, for the structural aspect of the theory of the subject.

The dividing line is the native limitation of the reversal. Because of this limitation, Sophocles' tragedy marks out antagonism in the power of the One. The point for Sophocles/Hölderlin is the retrogression toward the origin in its double aspect, the formal excess and the diffusion of the formless. In this case, the tragic hero owes his subjectivation to anxiety and his consistency to the superego — leading him to follow the involution of the ex-place to the point of death. The point for Aeschylus is completely different — it is the interruption of the power of origin and the division of the One. This interruption also has two aspects. The first is that of courageous refusal that questions the law under the effect of the excess-of-the-real and resolves anxiety by choosing the form of the *dispute*. (This takes place when Orestes demands that a decision be made on the question of whether he was right or wrong.) The other aspect is interruption and the reconstitution of a new order of justice. In neither case is the origin reinscribed in the new rule. Both aspects name the dimension of the subject that is always realized through the law (anxiety and the superego), but which is at the same time also in excess of it and enables it to constitute itself anew — in Aeschylus' case, as a new subject of the law.

As every great dialectician, Hölderlin at times recognized the value of Aeschylus: "And in patriotic reversal where the entire form of things changes, and where nature and necessity, which always remain, incline toward another form — be it that they transcend into chaos or into a new form."[20] However, the "new form" that could generate the tragedy can be realized only through death. Why? Because this new form is precisely the formal excess — it is the law itself caught in the vortex of terror. Chaos is nothing but the unlimited, as the proliferation of the formless. In fact, how can we apprehend the novelty of an effect if it is already subsumed within the mode of the native, in the absolute unity of the cause? Hölderlin also must allow for a principle of limitation — a total reversal, he says, is not granted to man. It is evident that a total reversal could not be native. For something like this to happen, we must be delivered from superegoic fixity. Aeschylus' model, in which courage and justice dialecticize anxiety and the superego, allows for divisibility and elucidates the possibility of deliverance. It is not that we have to leave the word "reversal" behind. Instead I want to distinguish two forms of it within the theory of the subject. First, there is the native reversal, which takes place in anxiety and pretends to cure, both through terror and its opposite, the mystical stupor. Then, there is the reversal of exile in which the denial of the old law and its internal division produces the illumination of the torsion inflicted upon the real (which takes the form of the new). The reversal of exile revokes the original as not-enough-real (*peu de reel*) and restores the real in justice. For this reason, it is a total reversal — it makes a *tabula rasa* of the past.

This is not simple: it is vain to hope that the process of the reversal of exile will take place without the structural support of the native, because it is from the materialistic impasse of the latter that the practical existence of the former proceeds. It is unilateral to declare the subject tragic; nevertheless, tragedy exists.

To sustain exile, or as Rimbaud says in *A Season in Hell*, "to stand one's ground" (*tenir le pas gagné*), is what Hölderlin could not do. Exile for him never stopped being the crucifying mediation of the return. There is no other definition of courage: it is precisely exile without return, the loss of the name. But Hölderlin wants to maintain the nomination of what is near: "And no wonder! Your native country and soil you are walking, / What you seek, it is near, now comes to meet you halfway."[21] We claim that it is necessary to overcome nostalgia, to excel in courage, the creative figure of return.

In Sophocles, we find that the quest is the return of the near in what is remote, the infinite patriotism of pure proximity, a truth so intimate that one has to die in order to uncover it in oneself. In Aeschylus, we find the remote in the near and exile in what is closest. Action performed on something whose logic is most foreign to us — this is the subject of antagonism. Even though we have to return — and it is this return that makes the subject — we have the chance to set free that which no longer calls for any return.

Translated by Marina de Carneri

The selection translated here is from "Manque et destruction," the third section of Alain Badiou's *Théorie du Sujet* (Paris: Éditions du Seuil, 1982).

1. Jacques Lacan, "Conférences et entretiens dans des universités nord-américaines," *Scilicet* 6/7 (1976): 15. [All quotations from this article are the editor's translation.]

2. Ibid.

3. Lacan, *The Seminar of Jacques Lacan, Book I: Freud's Papers on Technique, 1953-1954*, ed. Jacques-Alain Miller, trans. John Forrester (New York: Norton, 1988), 192.

4. Lacan, "Conférences et entretiens dans des universités nord-américaines," 32.

5. Ibid., 15.

6. Ibid.

7. Lacan, *The Seminar of Jacques Lacan, Book XI: The Four Fundamental Concepts of Psychoanalysis*, ed. Jacques-Alain Miller, trans. Alan Sheridan (New York: Norton, 1981), 163.

8. Ibid., 21.

9. Lacan, *Freud's Papers on Technique*, 102.

10. Lacan, *The Four Fundamental Concepts of Psychoanalysis*, 41.

11. Lacan, *Freud's Papers on Technique*, 198-199.

12. Ibid.

13. Ibid., 190-191.

14. Joseph Conrad, *The Nigger of the "Narcissus"* (New York: Norton, 1979), 145.

15. Baruch Spinoza, *Ethics* (New York: E. P. Dutton, 1938), 137.

16. Ibid., 126.

17. Aeschylus, *Eumenides*, trans. Christopher Collard (Oxford: Oxford University Press, 2002), 98-100.

18. Ibid., 103-105.

19. Friedrich Hölderlin, "Remarks on 'Antigone,'" in *Essays and Letters on Theory*, ed. and trans. Thomas Pfau (Albany: State University of New York Press, 1988), 110.

20. Ibid., 115.

21. Hölderlin, "Homecoming (To His Relatives)," *Poems and Fragments*, trans. Michael Hamburger (London: Anvil Press Poetry, 1994), 277.

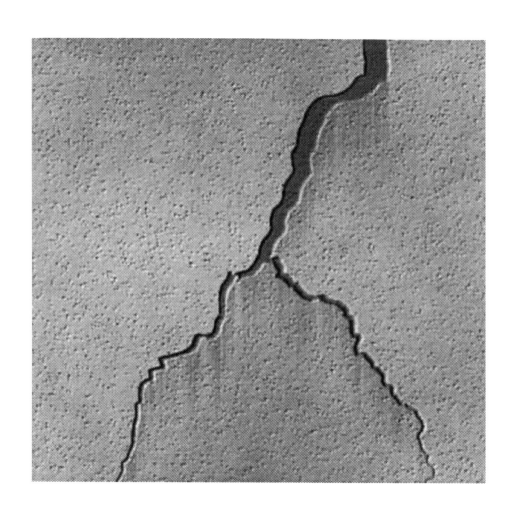

LACK OF BEING, DENIAL OF GOOD

candace vogler

*whether phobic, hysterical, or obsessive, neurosis
is a question that being raises for the subject*
— Jacques Lacan[1]

THE AIMS AND ETHICS OF PSYCHOANALYSIS

Lacan asks, "Should the theoretical and practical purpose of our [psychoanalytic] action be limited to the ideal of psychological harmonization?"[2] His answer: no. Lacan rejects the claims that psychoanalysis aims at cure, claims that would reduce psychoanalysis to "a form of psychological normalization [that] implies what might be called rationalizing moralization."[3] This would position analysts as "guarantors of the bourgeois dream" — necessarily *fraudulent* guarantors because "it is only too obvious that [the analysand's] aspiration to happiness will always imply a place where miracles happen."[4]

Fair enough. Lacanian psychoanalytic theory places the object of longing out of reach, in some only-ever-postulated instant before or beyond socially informed subjectivity. If the happiness that the analysand seeks requires putting longing to rest by securing the object, then happiness cannot be the achievable aim of any human undertaking, psychoanalysis included. But what of lesser satisfaction? What of the "individual comfort linked to that well-founded and legitimate function we might call the service of goods? Private goods, family goods, domestic goods, other goods that solicit us, the goods of our trade or our profession, the goods of the city, etc."[5] Curing (ordinarily middle-class) analysands would involve helping those discontent with the repetitive, stultifying deadness of severe neuroses become simultaneously alive to and satisfied by that measure of pleasure afforded by the goods of heteronormative middle-class life (or with *less* than that, if one's analysands are not in any position to claim the best things).[6] Psychoanalytic practice aimed at normalization looks suspiciously like cosmetic surgery *without* the quick results and *without* comparable success rates.[7]

It gets worse. Lacan conducted training analyses the same way he conducted other analyses (in some significant sense of "same" — analyses are, of course, otherwise unique), treating wanting to become an analyst as a kind of presenting problem. His concerns with the aim of analysis inevitably point with special concern to the aim of training analyses. His question is not whether it is worth it for an unhappy person to go into analysis in order to be able to inhabit a life that she has spent years putting into place for herself. He asks how undertaking to become a psychoanalyst might answer to a wish to earn a living by doing some good for others through a sufficiently interesting form of professional practice. Note that this question leaves it up to those who never entertain the thought of becoming analysts themselves to enter analysis or not, to stay a course or not, and to take or leave whatever individualized path of experience engagement in psychoanalytic speech situations might bring. Their interest is not the issue. The issue is: why hang out one's shingle for them? What sort of responsibility is involved in practicing psychoanalysis, given that the theoretical orientation is radically disarming (that is, if the theory that informs the practice is any guide, then one cannot know *exactly* what one is doing)? What sort of service do psychoanalysts render?

Lacan is very clear about what psychoanalysis does not do. The analyst does *not*:

1) teach the analysand to return to some kind of "natural," instinctual spontaneity in order to counteract neurotic deadness (or the florid sterility of psychosis, for that matter): "[I]n making [the instincts] the natural law of the realization of harmony, psychoanalysis takes on the guise of a rather disturbing alibi, of a moralizing hustle or a bluff, whose dangers cannot be exaggerated."[8]

2) enlist the aid of the superego in propping up the analysand's moral conscience and so prepare the analysand for a smoother social life: "It is possible that the superego serves as a support for the moral conscience, but everyone knows that it has nothing to do with the moral conscience as far as its most obligatory demands are concerned. What the superego demands has nothing to do with that which we would be right in making the universal rule of our actions."[9]

3) give the analysand tools for functioning smoothly in daily life; Lacan links this suggestion with conceiving psychoanalytic practice as that which supports life in the service of goods, and to a "morality of power" that is bound up in everydayness: "The morality of power, of the service of goods, is as follows: 'As far as desires are concerned, come back later. Make them wait.'"[10]

It is notoriously difficult to give a concise account of Lacan's positive view of the aim of psychoanalysis. It is unclear to me whether Lacan had a singular *account* to offer. If I understand him, the art of Lacanian psychoanalysis turns on taking advantage of disruptive episodes in psychoanalytic speech situations in order to brush up against the traumatic kernel never articulated in psychoanalytic speech. Any such kernel marks sites of bereavement in a very peculiar sense: nothing was in place to be lost. The analyst listens for the disruptiveness of a wound, puncture, or rupture where, initially, there was no smooth surface in place for the rupturing. Associative speech (together with gestures, movements, facial expressions, and silences — the matter of the psychoanalytic session) is composed of signifiers carrying something of the subject's relation to lack in the twisted insistence of the signifying chain, itself "the chain of a dead desire."[11] Such a chain works itself around and toward an empty signifier, a signifier of lack. This becomes a kind of nodal point for interpretation under certain circumstances. Whether we describe the result of interventions guided by openness to the negative spaces circumscribed by psychoanalytic speech as untying knots of desire, as tracking relations to jouissance and the drive, or as traversing the fantasy, the Lacanian analyst appears to be casting his net across emptiness — *real* emptiness (the difference in the shape of nets appears to be no more than different ways of construing the inarticulate in the disruption of psychoanalytic speech). What sort of service is that? How could there be an ethics of such a practice?

I will suggest that Lacanian practice points to a site of genuine ethical crisis: the evacuation of legitimate ethical authority in modernity. The sense in which active or potential analysands (in training or not) find themselves in the same boat, lack-of-being-wise, also suggests this: ethical groundlessness disturbs, and part of privilege is life in the throes of ethical groundlessness. Accordingly, Lacan's work charts the costs of groundlessness spectacularly, and any service rendered by the analyst will bear the weight of staging an encounter with both ontological and normative emptiness.

DENIAL

In his reading of *Civilization and Its Discontents*, Lacan puts his finger on the philosophical trouble with any ethics of psychoanalytic practice: "the good as such — something that has been the eternal object of the philosophical quest in the sphere of ethics, the philosopher's stone of all the moralists — the good is radically denied by Freud."[12] Even if we leave aside the question of whether or not "the good as such...has been the eternal object of the philosophical quest," it is still unclear how to understand *the good as such*. Lacan traffics in Kant's writings (where the good as such would be unconditional good), the text of Aristotle (where there could be no such thing as Kantian unconditional good), some Christian theology (where the good as such might be conditioned — good for man, good for angels — or might be uncreated), Sade (where thought about uncreated good seems to have shifted toward the demand that the person of God the Father respond), and other European writers of a more or less philosophical bent.

Traditionally, European philosophers who trafficked in the good as such would smuggle in god and revelation at some point. Christian ethics between the ancients and the moderns, for example, often involved thought about divine law promulgated through the ongoing creation (with the caveat that, while a god might command that one of us, say, sacrifice his only son, even a god couldn't make son-sacrifice a principle of law for created human life — there were limits to the laws the god could write into the book of nature). It is worth mentioning — if only because secular ethics has survived godlessness for so long that we may no longer recall how that worked — that views based on divine law *do* ground ethics in an appeal to good. In Christian moral philosophy, the whole structure of god's past gifts to men enters into thought about reason in human action. We can owe each other things directly, on such views, because we are joint participants in a form of social life made possible by the god's providential magnificence, which gives us a place in the world we share. Promises and gifts from the god structure that life. The hand of the god secures the goodness of the goods that shared life brings. Past-, present-, and future-directed practical considerations receive their due from the place we have in the larger, god-made scheme of things. While none of this guarantees individual happiness to those who struggle to be good in the course of their maturity, the struggle brings reward in the larger scheme of things. In Aquinas, for instance, what Denis Bradley calls "the natural endlessness of human nature"[13] insures that, however hard the lot of virtuous people in this life, and however many the mortal rewards of vice, it befits every man in a position to hear the word of god to struggle to meet the challenge of (theologically informed) ethics. One way of reading Lacan's point about Freud, then, is by saying that, in Freud, this sort of god is gone.

Nowadays, by unspoken gentlemen's agreement, North Atlantic intellectuals do not use revealed truths outside the confines of specifically religious intellectual activity (theological disputes, for example). More precisely, while we might mention such matters in the course of, say, deploring the impact of believers' activities, or else arguing that attacks on religious influence are misguided, we do not use doctrine as such. Whether or not the good as such "has been the eternal object of the philosophical quest in the sphere of ethics," contemporary North Atlantic philosophical ethicists *do* continue to rely upon thought about good. There is no contradiction involved in refusing to advert to doctrine while discussing good.[14] Secularism simply turns away from theological accounts that purport to ground ethics in uncreated good. I take it that this is obvious and untroubling to secular philosophers. Most of us managed to wrest ethics from the hands of gods when we learned to generalize standard undergraduate readings of Plato: the good cannot be good because it is god-beloved; rather, it must be god-beloved because it is good; otherwise, the regularities of good would be accidental or arbitrary. We cannot ground ethics on whims, even the whims of gods. For all that, we rely upon the discussion of good in thinking about the foundations of ethical practice.

Grounding ethics in good requires coming up with some account of the point of ethical practice that ties it to good. Just as secular ethicists take questions of good out of the hands of divinities, they take these questions out of the hands of mere human wanting. On any standard North Atlantic (neo- or post-) Kantian account of morality, for example, we have already left the sphere of morality when wanting has entered the picture.[15] The source of right action, the source of the rightness of right action, is not supposed to be a matter of satisfying wants (one's own, or those of one's cherished fellows). Take, for example, normal-person promise-keeping. "I am A-ing because I promised to A" is supposed to explain why you A when you'd prefer *not* to A, as when you explain leaving off doing something productive or pleasant in order to keep a dull appointment. Promises serve to get people to do things in the *absence* of any clear want to do them and in the *presence* of purposes that will be thwarted or delayed by promise-keeping. Elizabeth Anscombe makes the point this way:

> What ways are there of getting human beings to do things? You can make a man fall over by pushing him; you cannot usefully make his hand write a letter or mix concrete by pushing; for in general if you have to push his hand in the right way, you might as well not use him at all. You can order him to do what you want, and if you have authority he will perhaps obey you. Again if you have power to hurt him or help him according as he disregards or obeys your orders, or if he loves you so as to accord with your requests, you have a way of getting him to do things...Now getting one another to do things without the application of physical force is a necessity for human life, and that far beyond what could be secured by those other means.[16]

If I love you or fear you, then these facts about me will lead me to want to do what you would have me do. There is no need to get me to promise to do anything. You need only let me know what you would have me do, and if I can do it without unduly injuring myself, I will. I will do it for your sake if I love you. I will do it for my own sake if I fear you. Whatever the case, how things are between the two of us makes it possible for you to get me to do things. But if you are instead relying upon extracting promises to get me to do something, and if this technique is effective, then your strategy depends upon the assumption that sometimes people keep promises when acting on their word will involve thwarting or delaying some of their purposes. (Notice that, as Anscombe also pointed out, "one constantly has such purposes," that is, purposes that are defeated or delayed by promise-keeping.[17]) The problem of justifying duty in secular ethics, then, is the problem of grounding obligation understood in these terms. Anscombe suggests that there is some hope of touching ground by considering the way a practice like promising makes goods of social life possible — for example, by giving you some reason to expect that someone will do as he says when you have no reason to expect that the joint forces of love and fear would so incline him. In effect, this offers a task-based account of the point of ethical practice. We need ethics in order to accomplish shared tasks that belong to our lot as social beings. Ethics is the often individually costly means to a collective end.

Such accounts have three inherent sources of potential weakness. First, arguably, some of the very same qualities of practice and person that enable the attainment of excellent collective ends (for example, everyone doing his bit for the common weal), would seem to enable the attainment of hideous collective ends (everyone doing his bit for systematic feats of impersonal evil, such as bureaucratized genocide or the waging of an unjust war). Second, the account is only as good as the story about what is needed in a shared form of social life, which can, if pushed, make the account seem too finely tuned to the detail of particular social formations to support the ethical generally. And anyway, third, it is unclear that we need to resort to duty to give a principled account of non-accidentally sound social life. Non-specific threats, for instance, may be sufficient to get people to behave well enough often enough with each other (the threat of the random audit, for example, may keep many more people than will ever be audited reasonably honest when doing their U.S. federal income taxes).[18]

A task-based account of the point of an ethical practice places the practice in the service of social goods. Lacan — a man noted for keeping his word, by the way — *explicitly* removes the ethics of psychoanalytic practice from this sphere by both critiquing life in the service of goods and pointing out that the kinds of ordinary goods made possible for analysands through analysis are mere side effects. Denying that psychoanalysis aims at cure is tantamount to denying that it is, by its very nature, useful to life in the service of goods. It might seem as though this puzzling insistence involves some kind of idiosyncratic ethical stance tied to political fashions of the mid-twentieth century. Perhaps Lacan had a principled objection to middle-class life (rooted in some vaguely Marxist sympathies — they were common enough in those days), and laminated these sympathies to his account of psychoanalytic theory and practice. If this were the case, then analysts could help themselves to Lacanian techniques and theoretical insights, ignore the proclamations about cure, understand Lacanian psychoanalysis as one among many psychotherapeutic practices, and then evaluate its usefulness in light of its positive, life-enhancing results for analysands. In this sense, Lacan's denials would amount to thinly disguised appeals to his own ethical or political convictions. We could take them or leave them. I think that Lacan closes off this possibility. If I understand him, the insistence that psychoanalysis does not aim at normalization is rooted in a peculiarly austere insistence on psychoanalytic theoretical consistency and in how consistent theorization norms practice.

Lacan *agrees* with Freud about the absence of foundational appeals to good in psychoanalysis:

> The question of the Sovereign Good is one that man has asked himself since time immemorial, but the analyst knows that it is a question that is closed. Not only doesn't he have that Sovereign Good that is asked of him, but he also knows there isn't any. To have carried an analysis through to its end is no more nor less than to have encountered that limit in which the problematic of desire is raised.

> That this problematic is central for access to any realization of oneself whatsoever constitutes the novelty of the analysis. There is no doubt that in the course of this process the subject will encounter much that is good for him, all the good he can do for himself, in fact, but let us not forget what we know

so well because we say it everyday of our lives in the clearest terms: he will only encounter that good if at every moment he eliminates from his wishes the false goods, if he exhausts not only the vanity of his demands, given that they are all no more than regressive demands, but also the vanity of his gifts. [19]

Sovereign Good, the good as such, small goods, false goods — Lacan links the problematic of desire (relation to lack) to various forms of good, suggesting that the Big Absence is related to a lack of *something to do with good*. It isn't just that the god of Christian theological ethics has retreated from the scene of psychoanalysis; even the *secular* ground for ethics has fallen away. Not only do we find ourselves unable to appeal to doctrine, we lack a social task-based account of the good of psychoanalytic practice. We inherit a love-and-fear picture of the efficacy of social practices generally, of psychoanalytic practice in particular, and any good of psychoanalysis will be caught up in the good of tracing out the effects of the Big Absence in a life with no claim that such activity is otherwise, in any obvious way, socially useful.

DIAGNOSES

The easiest way to grasp the depth of the denial of good in Lacanian psychoanalysis is to step away from the texture of the seminar on ethics and consider Lacan's diagnostic categories. There are three of these — psychosis, neurosis, and perversion — and, in developing the grounds for differential diagnoses, Lacan provides a distinctively psychoanalytic account of the modes of modern subjectivity. This account offers a decided advance over Freud, taking up Freud's suggestion that there is no clear distinction between pathological and normal modes of psychic functioning and presenting a general account of the modern subject. There are many ways to discuss Lacanian diagnostic categories. Bruce Fink provides an especially elegant summary of some of them:

> Whereas the psychotic may suffer from what is experienced as an invasion of jouissance in his or her body, and the neurotic attempts above all to avoid jouissance (maintaining an unsatisfied or impossible desire), the pervert gets off on the very attempt to draw limits to his jouissance. Whereas in psychosis the Other does not exist (since its principal anchoring point, the Name-of-the-Father, is not instated), and in neurosis the Other exists only too ponderously (the neurotic wishing to get the Other off his or her back), in perversion the Other must be made to exist: the pervert has to stage the Other's existence by propping up the Other's desire or will with his own...Let us turn now to the mOther, the imaginary or real mother. In psychosis she is never barred by the Name-of-the-Father, and the psychotic never emerges from her as a separate subject; in neurosis she *is* effectively barred by the Name-of-the-Father, and the neurotic *does* emerge as a separate subject; in perversion the Other must be made to exist so that the mOther can be barred and the pervert can emerge as something other than an imaginary object of her desire. [20]

These three categories are very nearly exhaustive (there is some suggestion in Lacan's later work that it might be possible for the neurotic to attain a different relation to her or his world by traversing the fantasy — but this relation would not appear to have the characteristics of therapeutic "adjustment" in any usual sense of that term). If we step back from these categories (leaving to one side the possible fourth, which will not in any case repair the breach that I have tried to mark as the site where the god of St. Thomas left the scene and no account of social goods stepped into its place), something extraordinary appears.

The place of normative authority (moral, linguistic, or otherwise) in Lacan's diagnostic categories is occupied by the Other. As Slavoj Žižek reminds us, "[t]he topic of the 'other' must be submitted to a kind of spectral analysis that renders visible its imaginary, symbolic, and real aspects...First there is the imaginary other — other people 'like me,' my fellow human beings with whom I am engaged in mirrorlike relationships of competition, mutual recognition, and so on. Then there is the symbolic 'big Other' — the 'substance' of our social existence, the impersonal set of rules that coordinate our coexistence. Finally there is the Other qua Real, the impossible Thing, the 'inhuman partner,' the Other with whom no symmetrical dialogue, mediated by the symbolic Order, is possible."[21] It is clear enough that the secular philosophical problem of grounding ethics will find no solution in imaginary otherness. Imaginary otherness is just the domesticated, coherent, charted otherness of other people. The point of the puzzle about ethical grounding isn't, say, to figure out how to get other people to do things by getting them to say that they will. The point is, rather, to explain why anyone *should* abide by his word when he doesn't want to (given that he only needs to *give* his word when he does not expect to want to do it). Similarly, one form of symbolic otherness is the otherness of the moral rules by which we live. Pointing out that there *are* some rules cannot answer the philosophical question of whether we *ought to* follow them. *Real* otherness would thus have to be the place within which we sought something like ethical grounding. Unhappily, real otherness, for Lacan, far from giving the imprimatur of goodness to the rules we live by, is monstrous. It marks a limit that cannot be taken up into moral theory. Accordingly, the diagnostic categories take shape as subjective configurations in relation to desire, which is, on this view, a relation to lack, and one aspect of that lack is lack of normative grounding.

What does hearing the call of normative authority become on this picture? It amounts to a brush up against the profound *inadequacy* of the normative prohibitions that shape the emerging subject. Consider Lacan's description of the *successful* easing of Oedipal struggles:

> [T]he real father is elevated to the rank of Great Fucker — though not, believe me, in the face of the Eternal, which isn't even around to count the number of times. Yet doesn't this real and mythical father fade at the moment of the decline of the Oedipus complex into the one whom the child may easily have already discovered at the relatively advanced age of five years old, namely, the imaginary father, the father who has fucked the kid up.

Isn't that what the theoreticians of analytical experience say as they mumble away? And doesn't one find the point of difference there? Isn't it in connection with the experience of privation the small child undergoes — not because he is small but because he is human — in connection with what the child experiences as privation, that the mourning for the imaginary father is forged? — that is a mourning for someone who would really be someone. The perpetual reproach that is born at that moment, in a way that is more or less definitive and well-formed depending on the individual case, remains fundamental in the structure of the subject. It is this imaginary father and not the real one which is the basis of the providential image of God. And the function of the superego in the end, from its final point of view, is hatred for God, the reproach that God has handled things so badly.[22]

The figures of these fathers are partly products of Lacan's reading of *Totem and Taboo*. The real father, godlike, has access to all women. His murder installs the symbolic, the Name-of-the-Father as the mark of a mythical social compact built around the incest taboo (the incest taboo here has the status of the primary prohibition at the root of social order). The real father is a nonexistent, monstrous Other. The symbolic father occupies the dead zone that turns on installing the No/Name of-the-(dead)-Father in the child, and thereby writing the child as subject into the social order through prohibition. The imaginary father was the individual charged with performing the paternal function — installing the symbolic order through appropriate prohibitions, separating child from mother — and is, as mere person, inadequate to the task of legitimating this operation. He gets his way because he is bigger and stronger than the child and because the mother does not oppose him effectively. He is elevated, enshrined, worshipped, and hated through ego-ideals and superego orientation.

In this story, there is no such thing as a coincidence of voice of authority with authoritative source. There is no coincidence of prohibition and ethical ground. There is no social configuration that could underwrite its own rules. No mere mortal *could* fill the shoes of "someone who would really be someone." In short, there is no legitimate source of moral authority cut free from the love-and-fear modes of getting humans to do things. In Anscombe's useful sketch, this is tantamount to claiming that there is no source of moral authority. Notice that the philosophical puzzle about grounding morality cannot even be formulated coherently on this view — there is love, hate, and fear; there are commands and demands; there is privation and sacrifice; but there could not be a story about the force of the rules we live by cut free from the subjective ground of action. For my purposes, what is crucial about this picture is that middle-class ethical groundlessness lines up with the split in the subject instated at the entry point of the symbolic order. It is not just that there is privation; it is that the privation sets the subject in motion as a want-to-be in the face of groundless prohibitions. Subjects emerge from traumatic encounters that effect an apparent transmogrification of an economy of love and fear into an economy of duty. Because the transmogrification is a kind of parental conjuring trick, rooted in mere desire, it can never be complete or entirely successful. The suffering of analysands becomes a mark of the *groundlessness* of the very system that makes possible their emergence as subjects. There is "a lack in the Other, a lack inherent in the Other's very function as the treasure trove of signifiers. And this is so insofar as the Other is called upon (*ché voui*) to answer for the *value* of this treasure."[23]

Secular North Atlantic ethicists will doubtless protest that Lacan falls prey to a genetic fallacy. Even if it were true that some prohibitions were instated well before we reached the age of reason, and even if it were true that the voice of normative authority in most of our experience is nothing but the echo of a parental voice, this would in no way compromise normative authority. For example, while most middle-class people acquired toilet know-how well before they could think out the kind of good at issue in widespread reliance upon modern sewage disposal and treatment technologies, and while many of us will never wonder what it would be like if things were otherwise, the practice is *grounded* in considerations of collective health. We can offer a task-based account of the *point* of the practice even if no task-based rationale accompanied toilet training. We may be able to offer still more splendid accounts of why we *should* keep our word, tell the truth, refrain from hitting, and so on. Why shouldn't analysands leave the couch and take a course in moral theory instead of mistaking ethical prohibitions for groundless demands issued from the mouths of dubious sources?

Lacan seems never to entertain such an objection. I do not think that it can be formulated from inside his account anyway, which suggests that the account may be question-begging. Perhaps it is. There are, however, at least three reasons for not leaving the interior of the theory to answer the philosophical objection. First, if acceptance of some prohibition or requirement is rooted in an appeal to individual reason (or even an appeal to the bland common sense in task-based accounts of ethics), then a single mechanism — acceptance — will explain how you get both a sound *and* an unsound principle into you. (This is a cartoon version of one of Hegel's objections to the Kantian scheme — an objection that seems to me to underlie Lacan's magnificently perverse reading of Kant.) While this point is unlikely to move an obsessive (who is devoted to self-containment), it will certainly weigh with the rest of us. That a prohibition makes sense to you is no guarantee that it has a solid foundation. Accordingly, the fact that a modern subject has a prohibition in him *should not* be enough to satisfy him that the prohibition is sound, even if he is beholden to the prohibition.

Second, insofar as philosophical accounts of normative authority are meant to explain the felt weight or urgency of the call of duty, Lacan offers a compelling alternate account, one discovered through the history of psychoanalytic experience. For example, the desperation that a properly middle-class person experiences when she needs to go and no restroom is available is *not* an effect of the communal point of having waste disposal technologies in order. If her training was entirely successful, she may have trouble going outside even if she is in the middle of nowhere and the water table will not be threatened by her relieving herself, just this once, behind the bushes. From the point of view of justifying morality, things are on even shakier ground. Moral considerations famously leave people cold at times and may not provide the best account of some action even when the individual agent is hot for morality. Kant never tired of pointing out that it is impossible to tell, in one's own case or anyone else's, whether one does as one should from and for the sake of an ethical motive or from some other source (the dead weight of one's upbringing, for example). Since, as Lacan stresses repeatedly, a middle-class person's initial and defining access to ethical practice is in the hands of parents, both the substance and force of ethics enters into any individual person *through* another person. It is not as though ethics subsists somewhere else, waiting to come upon us. We are at the mercy of our caretakers. Even if the practices admit of some grander justification, the bit of the practice that informs my conduct, *as* it informs my conduct, may lack suitable justification. Consider the following: my father may have told me true things only by accident (he did not know they were true; he thought he was deceiving me; it was a cruel joke). I accepted what he said. It may be that others can see the grounds of the views, but the views are not mine because they are well founded. They are mine because my father told me so.

Moreover, third, a modern, secular, and democratic social order is *predicated* on the thought that determining what matters in life is an individual task, collectivized only to the extent that we have to get along with others who do not share our private sensibilities in these matters, and so must be minimally decent toward unsympathetic strangers. There is no uncontroversial, singular account of the good as such in secular ethics nowadays. This is, if you like, the *sine qua non* of liberal, democratic philosophical accounts of the rational grounding of ethical practice. Because secular, liberal philosophy throws the foundations of ethics back upon the shoulders of individuals, it is very much to the point to query the origins of basic ethical prohibitions and requirements in the individual soul.

On my reading of Lacan, some such question mark is at the heart of neurosis. The question neurosis poses to being is at one and the same time a question neurosis poses to purported sources of normative authority. If we are consistent in leaving it up to reasonably well-behaved people how they will answer that question, then their implicit insistence that it has not been adequately answered ought to weigh with us. Any hysteric worth her salt, at least, will suspect that producing moral theory is one technique among many devoted to placing thinly disguised demands on people, demands that are illegitimate, even if they are appealing and even if they won her allegiance long ago.

Small wonder that the hysteric finds it unbearable when voices of authority enjoy ordering people about. The hysteric goes right at the Other, insistently, disruptively demonstrating that the Other is lacking something. (Think of Freud's hysterics who seduced him into developing psychoanalysis as theory and practice only to demonstrate, repeatedly, that he missed their point.) Aggressive, hysterical doubt tends to carry a libidinal strategy in which the hysteric simultaneously sets herself up as the object of another's desire, and withholds herself from the other. The ambivalence of the operation makes a kind of sense if the lack of being is, at root, a lack of legitimate authority. Having a primary orientation toward debunking any claim to normative authority (epistemic or ethical) only works if something *else* will hold water. If nothing holds water, and if the only thing that can hold *you* is something that would hold water, you live from a relentlessly social stance of unanswerable challenge. You maneuver the lack out into the open. Meanwhile, your own position as a want-to-be cannot very well rest content in the newly exposed hole in the Other (now demoted to mere other). You succeed in forcing recognition of lack (often by presenting yourself as what might fill it) just in case there is no point in actually serving as the object that might fill it. Overlapping holes do not make a whole.

While the hysteric is willing to fade as a subject, to position herself as the cause of the Other's desire, she has a certain aversion to jouissance. Hysteria involves a complex parody of being and withholding an object on which the Other might get off. As Colette Soler puts it, "[t]he hysteric is someone who is always absent at the right moment, who always fails the partner." [24] But if the lacks in question line up along the normative vector that I have been describing, we could as easily say that the hysteric is someone who knows that there is no proper Partner, who acknowledges both her irreducible dependence on a partner and the fact that any partner will fail her, and who will be tempted always to head off that disappointment at the pass, all the while demonstrating the failure by exposing the lack in the Other.

The obsessive, by contrast, is content to get off on objects, but flees any hint that his objects are such because of their relation to the Other. Like his hysteric counterpart, he senses the lack in the Other. Unlike the hysteric, however, who takes some pleasure in enacting her various dramas of dependence (for example, in insisting that the failure is always on the side of the partner), he finds his dependence on the (inadequate) Other unbearable. If hysteria is discursive, social, and by its nature addressed to others, obsession is a kind of guilt-ridden, authority-saturated, rebellious monologue. The obsessive staves off the Other in order to avoid contact with the Other's desire/lack (again, registered psychically as a demand). Because obsession is isolating, propped up by an ill-concealed illusion of transparent self-adequacy, it wears its deadness on its sleeve. The hysteric is split, and from her lack turns to the Other; the obsessive, writes Soler, "manages to suture his subjective division." [25]

You can sense an obsessive cast to Descartes' Meditator in the fact that the Meditator thinks he can doubt the existence of any human person — his own included — under his own steam, but that he needs to postulate a malicious demon to make room to doubt the laws of arithmetic, the laws governing symbolic order. Notice that the Meditator is able to dissolve his demon postulate only by arguing that nothing *that* powerful could lack anything. Since it would *have* to lack something if it wanted to deceive him, the monstrous postulate *must* be false. Unlike the hysteric, the obsessive props up the Other by fleeing the possibility of its lack.

Meanwhile, the phobic (the third variety of neurotic) attempts to prop up the Other by making up some of the difference in an imperfectly performed paternal function (a lack of appropriate prohibition on the part of the father) by developing a rich symbolic system that turns on indeterminate fear of possible agents of the Law.[26] The pervert, for his part, goes through his whole maturity attempting to seduce the world into providing a law that he can respect. The quest is hopeless, of course, and the psychotic is lost in the whirl of invasion by imaginary otherness, having already foreclosed the question of legitimate authority.

Because psychosis, neurosis, and perversion are the *only* modes of modern subjectivity on this view, there is no way out of the joint (and mutually reinforcing) crises in being and authority in the Lacanian accounts of subjectivity. It is not the case that those of us who get by without ever thematizing the problem *have* something that analysands lack. Rather, we manage to hold at bay chronic absences at the center of things. Asking whether we might be better off for this is like asking whether the boy in the story would be better off pretending that the emperor was, in fact, wearing new clothes.

BY WAY OF A CONCLUSION

It is certainly true that all of the figures of modern subjectivity in Lacan suffer from a lack in being. I am urging that this lack in being involves, crucially, a crisis in authority.

The psychic strategies for coping with the crisis — sublimation, say, or the development of a strong superego that manages not to run amok[27] — involve casting one's lot with cultural constraints and developing effective screens against the blankness at the heart of the disconnected normative systems one inhabits serially and lives by more or less. In this sense, insisting that psychoanalytic practice serve the ends of heteronormalization does an injustice to both the theoretical insight gathered from the practice and the acuity of the mark of illegitimacy taken up in the psychic system of anyone in serious enough trouble to seek psychoanalysis. While analysands often exaggerate their difficulties, theirs is not mere psychic malingering. On Lacan's readings, analysands are in the grip of a crisis — a crisis in normative authority — that most of us are able to dodge most of the time. I take it that Lacan charts this crisis in a way that gives theoretical punch to Nietzsche's cry that god is dead by pointing to the ways in which psychoanalysis rests on a denial of the good as such.

The denial is no mere Freudian quirk inherited by generations of analysts from their atheistic founding father. Lacan reads the denial as itself a conclusion founded on the experience of psychoanalytic practice. The denial of good is a positive *gain* to psychoanalytic theory from psychoanalytic practice. Rat Man collapses when the Captain takes pleasure in inflicting pain, when the surrogate Other betrays an all-too-human desire. Little Hans' horse will bite or fall, injure or be injured, in incompatible dramas of power and impotence, and Hans makes up for the absence of effective paternal functioning by resolutely, fearfully spinning out a symbolic system that will not let the law go missing entirely. Anna O. swells up with Breuer's "child" at exactly the moment that Freud and Breuer are busily congratulating themselves on the effectiveness of their "talking cure" (as she names it for them). Schreber is at the mercy of a sex-crazed and abusive god. The classic analysands (whether known through the work of analysts in session or known only from their textual remains) — those figures from whom we learn the theory — teach Lacan that they bear witness in their suffering to an ongoing and acute crisis in normative authority. Their efforts to get the Other off their backs, or to bring the Other on board somehow, testify to the depth and severity of the crisis.

I realize that it is hard even to raise a serious question about normative authority these days. What makes it difficult to begin to address the psychoanalytic denial of good as such is that the authority question has a tendency to moot itself before it ever raises its head. In psychoanalytic work, the question moots itself whenever theorists are more inclined to diagnose the questioner than to answer the question. (On my reading, Lacan *does* diagnose the questioner rather than answering the question, but this is because he relies on the history of psychoanalytic findings to argue that the question has no answer, and that this *is* crucial to our topic.) More generally, most sufficiently cosmopolitan secular intellectuals either do not think that there could be any grounding for legitimate moral authority, or else assume that the basis for ethics involves the conditions conducive to non-accidentally sound human social life. Since what *counts* as non-accidentally sound human social life varies with the goods made possible and available by the relevant social formations, the latter approach looks to ground ethics in something like local color. The classic analysands could not rest content with this, and Lacan is faithful to them.

The first principle of an ethics of Lacanian psychoanalytic practice becomes a principle of fidelity to the coinciding absences in being and authority that shape subjectivity from its emergence and that are rendered acute in the suffering of analysands. Accordingly, refusing to see psychoanalysis as directed at promoting intrapsychic harmony amounts to refusing to downplay the impact of the crises in question. You can't *cure* lack of being. You can't cure lack of legitimating normative authority either. Analysands are not *wrong* to flee the brush against abyssal contact with such absences. The question is rather one about how to live with them, and I take it that Lacan's otherwise puzzling remarks about beauty, sublimity, comedy, and tragedy point to the precarious business of doing so. The relay from desire to jouissance to fantasy in the various descriptions of technique represent, on this reading, three strategies for remaining faithful to the problem in the service of non-destructive human vitality played out from some position other than demand, insistent subordination to a sense of lack, or moral high ground.

If I understand the possibility of a neurotic traversing the fantasy, going beyond neurosis, its trajectory will break the neurotic's submission to the Other, permitting complete separation. Separation could not answer the normative question, of course. Nevertheless, it may well ease the acuity of the crises of being and normative authority. Separation might, for example, put a halt to implicitly directing the normative and ontological questions to other individuals, thereby allowing the analysand the space needed to turn away from pointless efforts to conjure something that could repair the damage from the stuff of mere sociality. Turning away from the inherent, structural imperfections of an economy of desire toward satisfactions associated with the drives (which comprise a capacity to enjoy enjoyment) would certainly count as a kind of personal gain for a neurotic analysand. Whether and how it might count as a gain for ethics is another question, one Lacan leaves unanswered: "This is the beyond of analysis, and has never been approached."[28]

I am grateful to Jonathan Lear for extremely helpful comments on the penultimate draft of this essay.

1. Jacques Lacan, *Écrits: A Selection*, trans. Bruce Fink (New York: Norton, 2002), 159.

2. Lacan, *The Seminar of Jacques Lacan, Book VII: The Ethics of Psychoanalysis, 1959-1960*, ed. Jacques-Alain Miller, trans. Dennis Porter (New York: Norton, 1992), 302.

3. Ibid.

4. Ibid., 303.

5. Ibid.

6. See ibid., 303, 304, 305, 313-15, 318-19, 321, and 324.

7. Now, we might object that entering analysis is more like taking out an unusually expensive health club membership than it is like getting a face-lift. However, Lacan's remarks cast doubt on whether heteronormalization counts as "health," which is why it seems more apt to liken heteronormalization to the results of liposuction than to aerobic fitness.

8. Lacan, *The Ethics of Psychoanalysis*, 312.

9. Ibid., 310.

10. Ibid., 315.

11. Lacan, *Écrits*, 158.

12. Lacan, *The Ethics of Psychoanalysis*, 96.

13. As Bradley puts it, "the thrust of Aquinas's authentic doctrine...leads to an *aporia*: any moral philosophy inspired by Aquinas cannot legitimately return to a quasi-Aristotelian form of eudaimonism; but neither can it, as [secular] philosophy, go forward to a theological affirmation of man's ultimate supernatural end." Denis J. M. Bradley, *Aquinas on the Twofold Human Good: Reason and Human Happiness in Aquinas's Moral Science* (Washington, D.C.: Catholic University of America Press, 1997), xiii.

14. One way of understanding Lacan's insistence that psychoanalysis does not aim at normalization, for example, is as an insistence that normalization is not, as such, good. The point (that is, *the good*) of psychoanalysis is *not* that it aims at such an end. Rather, adaptation to one's life circumstances might be one side effect of psychoanalysis.

15. I use "wanting" to mark a distinction between contemporary North Atlantic mainstream philosophical accounts of the relevant aspect of motive and "desire" in a properly Lacanian sense of the term. The philosophers will take it that wanting relates us to objects, understood in any of several senses. The closest fit to this usage in Lacan comes through discussion of demand, not desire, and even there the overlap is not precise since demand is never fully articulated.

16. G. E. M. Anscombe, "On Promising and its Justice, and Whether it Need be Respected *in Foro Interno*," in *Ethics, Religion and Politics*, vol. 3, *The Collected Philosophical Papers of G. E. M. Anscombe* (Oxford: Basil Blackwell, 1981), 18.

17. Ibid., 19.

18. The most common philosophical technique for grounding ethics has nothing to do with the task-based approach; rather, it lies in grounding ethical practice in an appeal to individual rationality. The founding father of this approach is, of course, Kant, although there are very many neo-Kantian and some neo-Hobbesean approaches as well. The neo-Hobbesean approaches will fail only in the case of an individual who cares nothing for her own long-term well being and wants very much to injure as many people as she can while she's able, or who is boundlessly altruistic. In the former case, positive antisociality will defeat any appeal to it being in her interest to behave decently with her fellows. She will prefer to prey upon them, should the heavens fall. In the latter, she is already so willingly self-sacrificial in her dealings with her fellows that there is no reason for *them* to refrain from preying upon her. The neo-Kantian approaches depend upon such matters as our susceptibility to the call of others and to the insistence that we will to be only as happy as we are good. This is all well and good in a reasonably sound social formation with

reasonably sociable participants. Nevertheless: (1) even Kant thought that postulation in a divine order of justice was needed to render it reasonable to suppose that a virtuous and dutiful life would bring some happiness to the good man (a good soul is no insurance against natural or man-made catastrophe, after all) because (2) no individual can bring it about by her own actions that she inhabits a social world sufficiently well-ordered to provide a fitting context for the neo-Kantian appeal to reason. Since, moreover, the Lacanian analysand is acutely aware that no individual person could conjure up a sufficient guarantee of the soundness of a normative system, the appeal to individual reason ought not move her. What no one can do alone cannot be done through the mere aggregation of loci of individual practical reason, and certainly cannot be accomplished by stripping the agent down to a bare point of rationality, without an appeal to her own needs and wants or to the needs and wants of beings like her. The Lacanian analysand is not just involved in a Hegelian drama of intersubjective dependence. She is involved in a relay of intersubjective dependence in a system of relations that revolve around illegitimacy and lack.

19. Lacan, *The Ethics of Psychoanalysis*, 300.

20. Bruce Fink, *A Clinical Introduction to Lacanian Psychoanalysis: Theory and Technique* (Cambridge: Harvard University Press, 1997), 193-94.

21. Slavoj Žižek, "The Real of Sexual Difference," in *Reading Seminar XX: Lacan's Major Work on Love, Knowledge, and Feminine Sexuality*, ed. Suzanne Barnard and Bruce Fink (Albany: State University of New York Press, 2002), 70.

22. Lacan, *The Ethics of Psychoanalysis*, 307-308.

23. Lacan, *Écrits*, 303; emphasis added.

24. Colette Soler, "Hysteria and Obsession," in *Reading Seminars I and II: Lacan's Return to Freud*, ed. Richard Feldstein, Bruce Fink, and Maire Jaanus (Albany: State University of New York Press, 1996), 269.

25. Ibid., 274.

26. See Lacan's reading of Little Hans in *Le Séminaire de Jacques Lacan, livre IV: La relation d'objet, 1956-1957*, ed. Jacques-Alain Miller (Paris: Seuil, 1994), 212, 230, 245-46, and 284.

27. It is unclear, incidentally, how there could be a non-accidental way of keeping a strong superego tucked in enough to make life possible. On Lacan's reading, the Freudian superego — the mode of psychic disruptiveness that insists in the name of some misplaced law — will not let up. "According to Lacan," writes Žižek, "this 'feeling of guilt' [associated with superego] is not a self-deception to be dispelled in the course of the psychoanalytic cure — we really *are* guilty: superego draws the energy of the pressure it exerts upon the subject from the fact that the subject was not faithful to his desire, that he gave it up. Our sacrificing to the superego, our paying tribute to it, only corroborates our guilt. For that reason our debt to the superego is unredeemable: the more we pay it off, the more we owe" (*The Metastases of Enjoyment: Six Essays on Woman and Causality* [London: Verso, 1994], 67-68). Through an extraordinary misreading of Kant (a performed, elaborate misunderstanding of Kantian moral law worthy of a theorist of the superego, perhaps), Lacan at once analogizes the operations of the Kantian motive of duty to the operations of the Freudian superego *and* denies that the Freudian superego is a capacity for ethical or moral agency. Instead, the superego is a residue of Oedipal compromise, an insistent, unreconciled disruptiveness that catches and perpetuates the tone of voice that lays down the law and enjoys the business of prohibition — wildly, gleefully promulgating law, often in retrospect, for the sake of the guilt. Accordingly, superego operation is not particularly beholden to the limits and permissions of customary ethics. Its alibis ("You have to do this for your own good," "You owe this to the group," "This hurts you more than it hurts him," for example) are just that — alibis. The Kantian categorical imperative becomes: Enjoy. The disaster is that there are no clear and principled limits on this enjoyment.

28. Lacan, *The Seminar of Jacques Lacan, Book XI: The Four Fundamental Concepts of Psychoanalysis*, ed. Jacques-Alain Miller, trans. Alan Sheridan (New York: Norton, 1981), 273.

LACAN AT THE LIMITS OF LEGAL THEORY:
LAW, DESIRE, AND SOVEREIGN VIOLENCE

steven miller

CIVIL DISOBEDIENCE AND THE LAW OF GOD

The best place to seek the concept of law is not in the theory of law itself but in the praxis of civil disobedience. More than a political strategy, civil disobedience manifests — or rather "demonstrates" — the disjunction between the existence of the law and its essence, that is, between the existence of an unjust law and the essence from which this law should derive its authority. This disjunction has been articulated primarily in terms of the dualism of natural law theory, which holds that any given terrestrial law ("the law of the land") ultimately derives its authority from the law of God or the moral law. The clearest theoretical presentation of the connection between civil disobedience and the law of God occurs in Martin Luther King, Jr.'s theologico-political epistle, "Letter from Birmingham City Jail":

> One may well ask, "How can you advocate breaking some laws and obeying others?" The answer is found in the fact that there are two types of laws: there are *just* and there are *unjust* laws. I would agree with Saint Augustine that "An unjust law is no law at all."

> Now what is the difference between the two? How does one determine when a law is just or unjust? A just law is a man-made code that squares with the moral law or the law of God. An unjust law is a code that is out of harmony with the moral law...Any law that uplifts human personality is just. Any law that degrades human personality is unjust. All segregation statutes are unjust because segregation distorts the soul and damages the personality.[1]

In this context, the law of God has a strictly political importance; it is the name for the principle of justice (universal equality and liberty) whereby terrestrial laws can be legitimately contested. For King, in accord with the tradition of Kantian-Christian morality, this principle is inseparable from the sanctity of human personality; every law must recognize the inviolability of human personality in order to be recognized as a law of the land. Rather than standing for a value unto itself, however, the primary value of what King calls the "moral law" inheres in its function as a test of the lawfulness of positive law. The moral law can thus be reduced to the "virtue" or "sense" of justice — reduced, in other words, to the categorical imperative that unjust laws must always be actively contested. The famous opening lines of John Rawls' *A Theory of Justice* (written contemporaneously with the civil rights struggles of the 1960s) articulate just such an imperative: "Justice is the first virtue of social institutions, as truth is of systems of thought. A theory however elegant and economical must be rejected or revised if it is untrue; likewise laws and institutions no matter how efficient and well-arranged must be reformed or abolished if they are unjust. Each person possesses an inviolability founded on justice that even the welfare of society as a whole cannot override."[2] If virtue is the political actualization of morality, then civil disobedience would be the political act that manifests the sense of justice.

The absolute value of the person, however, need not be the only test of the lawfulness of the law, just as the meaning of civil disobedience need not depend upon reference to such a value. This form of political action has an import that goes beyond its theoretical justification. Civil disobedience remains a decisive and relevant practice because it manifests the possibility of legitimate contestation — the contestation of unjust state action — that does not depend upon deference to a sacred principle (be it the Good, the Person, or the Law, along with their historical corollary, the economy of private ownership). Indeed, it is my initial working hypothesis that the question of law cannot even be posed as such until it is emancipated from its traditional complicity with the economy of personhood and private ownership. On this point, my discussion follows certain basic theses of the legal thought of both Hans Kelsen and Jacques Derrida.[3] The works of these seemingly incompatible thinkers are linked through their fidelity to the Kantian tradition — or rather, through their attempt to inherit the Kantian tradition in a way that takes it beyond its entrenchment in the values of personhood and property.[4]

The attempt to think such an emancipation of law from the property system involves two major difficulties. First, *contestation*: if the law can no longer be conceived on the basis of its adherence to a transcendent principle, what is the basis for its legitimate contestation — that is, a possible contestation of legalized injustice that does not abrogate fidelity to the rule of law as such? In the name of what does one contest injustice if not the inviolability of the person and his property? Second, *violence*: the price of affranchising the question of the law from its complicity with a legal system designed to protect private property is a more complex engagement with the relation between law and violence. Kelsen's theory is exemplary on this point: he holds that the only possible concept of law, a concept that would transcend the relation between juridical institutions and specific politico-economic systems (capitalist or communist), would be a concept that defines law according to the horizon of its enforcement, that holds the force of law to be intrinsic to law as such. As such, for Kelsen, law is what he calls a "coercive norm."[5] Derrida makes an analogous argument: he elaborates both the genealogy, from Montaigne and Pascal to Kant, and the political horizon of such a concept of law as the "force of law."[6]

In contemporary political thought, the answer to the first set of difficulties takes the form of an attempt to discover if the *universal* has a place beyond the theological determination of politics, and thus to think the universal in terms of the contestation of personality, the division of the subject, the death of God, expropriation, or arche-violence. The second set of difficulties is linked to the first through the question of civil disobedience. The wager implied in the traditional praxis of civil disobedience is that the violence of law — and even the most revolting implementation of this violence in the form of "law enforcement" — presupposes such a universal. The wager is that *this* law, no matter how unjust, can only ever be enforced as *the* law — that the active enforcement of *a* law (the law of a specific land) necessarily implies the claim that it is *the* law and thus universal. In the case of an unjust or discriminatory statute, the enforcement of the law will always entail a presupposition that contradicts the letter of the law. At the moment of enforcement, the state can no longer avoid the universality presupposed by the fact of its own institutions, and thus unavoidably exposes itself to claims that contest their justice.

The legitimacy of civil disobedience does not ultimately depend upon the principle that the act claims to uphold, but rather inheres in the specific theater of its public gesture. On the one hand, as Rawls writes in his chapter on the topic, the act of civil disobedience "addresses the sense of justice of the majority of the community"[7]; it openly insists on the disjunction between the existing laws and the law of law. On the other hand, the same act has a scope that exceeds the open airing of a principle of justice. Its function is not to transform the community into a theater of the beautiful soul, to represent an exclusive adherence to a law that transcends the law of every land. The paradoxical "civility" of civil disobedience inheres in the fidelity of this public action not to a higher law, but to the very same unjust law of the land that it openly disobeys. The gesture that represents such fidelity is in fact the most dramatic moment in any act of civil disobedience: the moment at which the actors submit to the legal consequences of their action, allowing themselves to be arrested. As Rawls writes, "[c]ivil disobedience...expresses disobedience to law within the limits of fidelity to law, although it is at the outer edge thereof. The law is broken, but fidelity to law is expressed by the public and nonviolent nature of the act, by the willingness to accept the legal consequences of one's conduct."[8] Beyond demonstrating the contradiction between the law of God and the law of the land, the theater of civil disobedience would thus body forth this other contradiction between the universal implied by law enforcement and the discrimination written into the law or otherwise manifest in state action. This activist "willingness to accept the legal consequences of one's conduct" displays an adherence to the sheer *fact* of the law beyond the set of its specific dictates.

For Rawls, this fidelity to law remains subordinate to the task of addressing the community, to the expression of conscience. To some extent, he advocates a kind of "responsible" activism, designed both to advance its claims and to reassure the state that disobedience is neither an act of war, juvenile resentment, or pathological compulsion, but is rather "conscientious and sincere." To accept the legal consequences of one's conduct (arrest, bodily injury) would thus function as a pledge of allegiance to the rule of law as such, that the act for which one is being punished has been undertaken in the name of a sense of justice (or even "a theory of justice"): "This fidelity to law helps to establish to the majority that the act is indeed politically conscientious and sincere, and that it is intended to address the public's sense of justice. To be completely open and non-violent is to give bond of one's sincerity, for it is not easy to convince another that one's acts are conscientious, or even to be sure of this before oneself."[9] It is important to be clear on this point: fidelity to law — to the rule of law or the mere fact of law — does not necessarily imply allegiance to constituted authorities, but rather to the possibility of contestation from which such authorities derive their own claims to legitimacy. The rule of law does not name the sovereignty of the prevailing order, but rather the point at which sovereign power *loses control of itself* — both in the sense that, in defense of unjust laws, state violence becomes constitutively illegitimate and excessive, and in the sense that it is at precisely the point of such excess that state action unavoidably exposes itself to contestatory interventions.

In the courtroom, the oath invokes the law of God as the guarantor of the truth. In the theater of civil disobedience, Rawls claims that one would "invoke" one's own present acquiescence to punishment (for example, going limp upon seizure by the police) as an attempt to guarantee ("to give one's bond") that one acts in accordance with the law of God itself. This is precisely the rhetorical situation of King's letter written from prison. In other words, civil disobedience presents a situation in which God is not the ultimate guarantee, a situation in which one must establish one's credibility and sincerity according to an immanent criterion in order to make others believe that one truthfully acts in the name of God or a rational sense of justice. This criterion is what Rawls calls simply "fidelity to law," but would more appropriately (and problematically) be called fidelity to the consequences of law, fidelity to the "force of law," or even fidelity to the violence of law. The disobedient protester does not simply contest state violence in the name of a higher principle of nonviolence, but rather openly (and contemptuously?) "swears" on the violence to which he submits at the very moment he is acting out of respect for a higher law.[10] The force of law thus opens a space in which it becomes possible to claim adherence to a universal principle, in which it becomes possible to expose one's adherence to the universal *as* universal, rather than as an unverifiable private predilection. Indeed, the universal only becomes thinkable within the horizon opened with such exposition.

THE FULFILLMENT OF THE LAW

Civil disobedience thus manifests an unavoidable and fundamental engagement with the law, without this law being reducible either to the statutes of a determinate legal order or to a law that transcends all legal orders. The law at stake emerges rather at the point where the "sincerity" of the act turns into a theatrical ironization of violence. It is not a coincidence, therefore, that the law in this sense should occur as a poetic *topos*.

One of Schönberg's choral song cycles (*Sechs Stücke für Männerchor*, op. 35), from 1930, includes the following lyrics:

> That there is a law
> which all things obey
> the way you follow your Lord:
> a law which is master of all things the way
> your Lord is your master:
> this is what you should recognize as a miracle!
> That someone decides to rebel
> is an obvious banality.[11]

These lines not only reduce the act of rebellion against the law to the status of banality, but also implicitly expose the limits of any theoretical attempt to elaborate a concept of law as such. The tonality of exhortation in general arises from a rupture — in this case, that rupture with the regime of sufficient reason called the "miracle." Accordingly, this exhortation asks its addressee to accept this rupture as the condition for thinking the law. It asks one to begin with the illegitimate fact of a law without concept.

Any discourse that attempts to theorize the law will be beset by the suspicion that its ultimate purpose is to uphold the preservation of an illegitimate and coercive legal system. When speaking of the law, one opens oneself to the accusation that this term represents merely the aspiration of a specific system of law to legitimate status, that one keeps an entire penal code in reserve for those who need convincing in order to accept that *this* law is *the* law. To speak of *the* law is always illegitimate simply because there is no such thing: there are only *laws* in the plural whose aspiration to the status of law will always be infinitely contestable. This plurality of laws, however, does not in itself invalidate the claim of each law or system of law to be lawful, does not make it impossible for each law to present itself as *the* law. On the contrary, this plurality is irreducible because *the* law is nothing other than the mere fact — the miracle of which Schönberg's song urges us to recognize — "that there is *a* law." Law as such thus becomes inseparable from the withdrawal of the concept or principle of law, from the fact that there is a law beyond any access to what law is. What Schönberg calls the "miracle" of the law's existence would thus name its essential excess, the event of its presentation beyond its own concept. The decision to rebel thus becomes a banality, amounting to nothing other than the claim that a given law is illegitimate because it has no right to call itself law, while such illegitimate nomination is in fact inseparable from the structure of law as such.

The same problems arise when one attempts to take up the philosophical question, "What is the law?" On the one hand, the question seems to refer to the essence of law or the concept of law. On the other hand, this version of the question will always be displaced by another. To ask "What is the law?" can always amount to asking "What is the law that applies to this case?"

"What does the law *say* in this situation?" Further, the problem of what the law says is not limited to knowing which law applies in any particular case, but extends to the problem of understanding what the specific applicable law means. Indeed, it is possible to become so absorbed with knowing what the law says that the question of its essence is indefinitely deferred, if not forgotten. The miracle of the law, therefore, would not so much occur as an epiphany before which one stands paralyzed with wonder; rather, it would lie in this engaged relation to the saying — the "juris-diction" — that will have always carried the law beyond the question of its essence.

What both the Jewish and the Christian traditions call *the fulfillment of the law* names the way in which this engaged relation to the saying of the law has always already been folded into the law itself. According to one rabbinical tradition, for example, Moses does not only deliver the Torah to the Israelites at Mount Sinai, but at the same time he is also supposed to have "revealed" to them every eventual commentary on the Torah and all the commentaries upon those commentaries.[12] The commentary on the saying of the law, in other words, comes "before the law" itself. Saint Paul predicates the Christian event upon the same tradition when he postulates that love for the neighbor is the fulfillment of the law: "The commandments, 'You shall not commit adultery; You shall not murder; You shall not steal; You shall not covet'; and any other commandment, are summed up in this word, 'Love your neighbor as yourself.' Love does no wrong to a neighbor; therefore, love is the fulfilling of the law" (Rom. 13:8-10). Paul departs from the rabbinic tradition only to the extent that he emancipates the relation to the law from the historical revelation of the law itself (from the tradition of Sinai). Instead, he finds the relation to the law in the praxis of love for the neighbor: love *does* no wrong to the neighbor. The law is "revealed" in the love for the neighbor, and this love reveals itself as the "miracle" of an engagement with the law (its "summation") that is both "older" and "newer" than the gift of the law itself.

DIVINE VIOLENCE

If the attempt to present *a* law as *the* law can never be upheld without reference to a coercive or punitive power, the point of the decision to rebel would be to contest this power (especially in cases where its deployment is manifestly unjust). The problem with such rebellion, however, is that it presumes the possibility of purifying law of its association with sovereign power. It can only contest the injustice of the power that is supposed to uphold the law in the name of the law "itself," or rather, in the name of the pure principle of a law whose legitimacy would not be contaminated by an appeal to violence. In other words, acts of rebellion remain effective only so long as they engage determinate systems of law, acts for which the responsible parties can be prosecuted. But such acts would lose their basis if a punitive violence, perhaps even of the most extortative variety, were inseparable from the pure concept of law as such — if this concept were nothing other than a "fact" to whose acceptance there is no alternative but the pain of death.

In "The Temptation of Temptation," his Talmudic lesson on the relation between law and reason, Emmanuel Levinas elaborates a tradition according to which the horizon of coercion and punishment emerges inseparably from the original gift of the law itself. Levinas' text is devoted to a passage from the Tractate *Shabbat* (88*a* and 88*b*) that comments on the simple lines of Exodus 19:17: "Moses brought the people out of the camp to meet God. They took their stand at the foot of the mountain." But the Talmudic passage immediately reinscribes these lines within a kind of rabbinical fiction that opens the horizon of a divine violence. Yahweh threatens to destroy his own people, using the mountain itself as an implement, if they decide not to accept the law that he presents to them. Rabbi Abdimi bar Hama bar Hasa comments that the lines from Exodus "teach us that the Holy One, Blessed be He, inclined the mountain over them like a titled tub and that He said: If you accept the Torah, all is well; if not here will be your grave." The miracle "that there is a law" thus happens as a violent extortion that divides the life of the people to whom the law is delivered. The revelation of the law only becomes a historical event to the extent that the very life of the people suddenly depends entirely upon its acceptance. The threat of divine violence places the Israelites in the position of making the impossible choice between the law and their own extinction.

For Levinas, however, this decision is not simply a forced choice because it occurs before it becomes possible to distinguish between freedom and coercion (unless the "force" in the forced choice names precisely the status of force or violence beyond their determination according to the distinction between freedom and coercion). One significant section of his reading revolves around the apparently nonsensical promise, which the Israelites were supposed to have offered Yahweh once he presented them with the law: "we will do and we will hear." The nonsense of the promise inheres in its inversion of a normative temporal order that the divine commandment generally functions to preserve. To the extent that the commandment prescribes certain deeds that should follow its word, it also prescribes in general that the deed as such should follow the word, that the deed is only possible based on a clear preliminary understanding of the word, and further, based on the presupposition that the word is inherently understandable. Conceived in this way, the form of the commandment inscribes the primacy of reason with respect to the law, the primacy of metalanguage with respect to language. How, then, could one *do* the law without first having *heard* its requirements, or without having scrutinized the ground for its claim to adherence? If this inversion takes place, it would pertain to the horizon of divine violence. Levinas elaborates the praxis that pertains to this inversion in terms of the fulfillment of the law: "To receive the gift of the Torah — a Law — is to fulfil it before consciously accepting it…Not only does acceptance precede examination but practice precedes adherence. It is as if the alternatives liberty-coercion were not the final ones, as if it were possible to go beyond the notions of coercion and adherence due to coercion by formulating a 'practice' prior to voluntary adherence."[13] The gift of the law is already the fulfillment of the law; the miracle of the law lies in its being accepted without being understood; the fact of the law lies in an act that goes beyond freedom and beyond the will.

Saint Paul's elaboration of "the fulfillment of the law" can be read as both an extension and a transformation of the same tradition. The love for the neighbor fulfills the law in that it constitutes a fundamental praxis from which the authority of the commandment itself would derive. What distinguishes the Christian love for the neighbor from the tradition from which it emerges, however, is that this love moves beyond the threat of every possible violence upon the life of the one to whom the law is addressed. Paul thus opens the trajectory, which culminates in Kant, that makes love for the neighbor into the movement whereby law is gradually detached from the possible enforcement that remains associated with the event of its revelation, a movement that ultimately leads beyond the form of the commandment itself. *Rather than commanding what cannot be done, the prescription to love the neighbor commands what can only be done without being commanded.* "Love *does* no wrong to a neighbor; therefore, love is the fulfilling of the law." The impossibility of the command paradoxically bears witness to a fundamental stratum of possibility, what Kant calls the "practicability" or even the "feasibility" (*Tunlichkeit*) of the moral law.[14] Even where the command has been articulated, the praxis of love itself should always have come before the law that makes it imperative: "For, as a commandment [to "*Love God before all, and your neighbor as yourself*"] it requires respect for a law that *commands love* and does not leave it to one's discretionary choice to make this one's principle. But love for God as inclination (pathological love) is impossible, for he is not an object of the senses. The same thing toward human beings is indeed possible but cannot be commanded, for it is not within the power of any human being to love someone merely on command. It is, therefore, only *practical love* that is understood in that kernel of all laws."[15] Love thus becomes synonymous with an ethical courage: one must always love without fear for one's life. Love is not love that admits the extortion of the violence that subtends every commandment. At the limit, such true unforced love (even the love of God himself) necessarily entails the death of God since its horizon exceeds the reach of his power. If the death of God shows that death itself has an omnipotence beyond the power of divine violence, then love belongs to the horizon of death.

LACAN AND THE DEATH PENALTY

Lacan locates the facticity of *the* law (the fact that there is *a* law) in analytic experience: "The hard thing we encounter in the analytic experience is that there is one, there is a law."[16] If the rudiments of a legal theory could be found in Lacan's writings, they would thus be largely consistent with the tradition that accepts the "hard thing" (or the "miracle") that "there is a law" without concept and without theory, and that makes this thing itself the basis for the contestation of injustice. Moreover, like Levinas, Lacan finds that this "hard thing" is inseparable from a sovereign violence, and he shows that this violence emerges where the law itself can no longer account for its own existence.

Despite readings that emphasize its analysis of the moral law, Lacan's "Kant with Sade" is as much an engagement with questions of positive legality. According to a tradition that conceives law as divided between these two — moral and positive — poles, Lacan never examines questions of the former without measuring their impact upon the paradigm of the latter. Although the reading of the *Critique of Practical Reason* and its determination of the "doctrine of virtue" belong to the explicit program of Lacan's essay, it also implicitly opens the way for an elaboration of the relation between psychoanalysis and the problems of legal institutions that pertain to the "doctrine of right." Indeed, the proper names invoked by the title itself might well bear witness to such a concern with both major divisions of the *Metaphysics of Morals*: whereas Lacan makes Kant into the name for the determination of the subject by the moral law, he makes Sade into the name for the institution of the moral law as the foundation of right and the possibility of justice. The perverse virtue of the Sadian maxim is not only to introduce the division of the subject (*enoncé, enonciation*) there where this division is repressed in Kant by the voice of conscience, but also to introduce the claim upon a *right* there where Kant limited himself to positing a *fact*, that is, the moral law as the "fact" of reason that constitutes the inviolable dignity of the person. In other words, Sade shows that even this universal fact takes place within the horizon of sovereign violence; he demonstrates that, politically speaking, a systematic and potentially infinite *violation* (jouissance) can occupy the place of what Kant calls dignity. The challenge of Sade is his claim that the universal is inseparable from violation and thus that jouissance is inseparable from the possibility of justice. Lacan responds to this challenge by revising both Kant and Sade. On the one hand, he locates the fact of law in desire rather than reason; on the other, like Sade (but also Levinas) he situates this fact within a sovereign violence. For Sade, sovereignty lies in the freedom of transgression, but the sovereignty that matters for Lacan is manifest in the cruelty of the death penalty. Whereas the sovereignty of transgression inheres in the violation of the law, Lacan shows that the death penalty is a paradoxical corollary of Christian charity, and thus that its sovereignty inheres in the fulfillment of the law. Lacan reinscribes this fulfillment as the "autonomy" of desire.[17]

In a discussion of censorship from his seminar of 1954-1955, Lacan examines a law that is formally analogous to the ultimatum that Yahweh delivers to the Israelites. Lacan addresses what he calls a "primordial law": "any man who says that the King of England is an idiot will have his head cut off."[18] The law is primordial because it excludes the position from which its acceptance could be the result of a deliberative act. The death penalty is thus the point at which the possibility of such an act is excluded. The law is accepted to the precise extent that its non-acceptance entails the death of its addressee.

> I want to show you that any similar law, any primordial law, which includes the specification of the death penalty as such, by the same token includes, through its partial character, the fundamental possibility of being not understood. Man is always in the position of never completely understanding the law, because no man can master the law of discourse in its entirety.

> I hope I'm giving you a feeling of this final, unexplained, inexplicable mainspring upon which the existence of the law hangs. The hard thing we encounter in the analytic experience is that there is one, there is a law. And that indeed is what can never be completely brought to completion in the discourse of the law — it is this final term that explains that there is one. [*Et c'est bien ce qui ne peut jamais être complètement achevé dans le discours de la loi — c'est ce dernier terme qui explique qu'il y en a une.*][19]

How does Lacan's version of the death penalty differ from the divine violence that Levinas locates in the rabbinical tradition? The answer to this question can be found in the closing pages of "Kant with Sade": the sovereign violence of the death penalty emerges on the far side of the commandment to love the neighbor. It is, as Lacan writes, "one of the corollaries of Charity."[20] In other words, the death penalty is the sovereign violence that survives the death of God, that goes beyond the divine violence which binds the people to the law. The death penalty is also a violence that binds one to the law, but, whereas divine violence comes from the same God who gives the law itself, the death penalty would come from a different god — or it would name, rather, the sovereign power of death itself freed from reference to any determinate authority. Whereas Yahweh threatens his people with the death that he has the power to administer, the recourse to the death penalty amounts to the deployment of death itself as a power. Although the death penalty remains inseparable from the incomprehensible fact that there is a law, it has a scope that far exceeds the limits of this fact. For Lacan, the problem of the death penalty only emerges with the fulfillment of the law in the love for the neighbor. In fact, following Freud, he describes this roving death as the repressed truth of the love for the neighbor — such that it becomes possible for him to understand the fulfillment of the law starting from the death penalty rather than from love. Rather than the revelation of the law in its praxis, the fulfillment of the law thus exposes the dimension of a sovereign violence that is irreducible to the law. The fulfillment of the law exposes that the fact of the law does not belong to the horizon of the law, and thus what Lacan calls *ethics* corresponds to the fulfillment of the law in this sense.

These considerations might help to measure the complexity of Lacan's assessment of Sade's position in the last pages of "Kant with Sade." Lacan's basic point is that, despite Sade's systematic apology for transgression and destruction, the logic of his demonstration remains bound to what Saint Paul called the "curse of the law." Lacan limits himself entirely to the closed set of "opportunities" opened by the explicit prohibitions (rather than the mere fact) of the law. The logic of the argument thus gestures toward that fulfillment in which tradition upholds the event of a miraculous rupture with this malediction:

> Sade thus stopped, at the point where desire is knotted together with the law. If something in him held to the law, in order there to find the opportunity Saint Paul speaks of, to be sinful beyond measure, who would throw the first stone? But he went no further.

> It is not only that for him as for the rest of us the flesh is weak, it is that the spirit is too prompt not to be lured. The apology for crime only pushes him to the indirect avowal [*aveu détourné*] of the Law. The supreme Being is restored in Maleficence.[21]

This avowal of the law does not amount to a confession of sin. Lacan is not saying that Sade's apology for crime ultimately becomes an elaboration of guilt and thus a personal appeal for forgiveness. The apology for crime as such can only be an avowal of the fundamental sin of subjection to the law and an appeal for expiation from this sin — an appeal, in other words, for expiation from the malediction of the law itself. In this sense, the avowal of the law restores the supreme Being to the extent that it functions as a demand perhaps addressed to the power of what Walter Benjamin calls "divine violence," which constitutes a form of retribution that "purifies the guilty, not of guilt, however, but of law." "For with mere life," Benjamin writes, "the rule of law over the living ceases. Mythical violence is bloody power over mere life for its own sake, divine violence pure power over all life for the sake of the living."[22]

For Lacan, however, the confession that appeals to the power of such expiation implies a disavowal of what Schönberg called the *miracle* of the law, what Kant called the *fact* of the moral law, or what Lacan himself (in the last lines of "The Subversion of the Subject and the Dialectic of Desire," which immediately follows "Kant with Sade" in the *Écrits*) called "the Law of desire." *Desire is the facticity of the law from which expiation is not possible.* (And the dictum from the *Ethics* seminar, "do not give up on your desire," would have a similar status to Schönberg's exhortation). The death penalty is the point at which the possibility of such expiation definitively withdraws. The fulfillment of the law toward which Lacan's analysis of Sade gestures would be nothing other than the mere presentation of the law beyond expiation.

Much like Saint Paul, Lacan situates the "Christian commandment" ("love your neighbor as yourself") beyond the logic of transgression to which the curse of the law restricts the subject. And he makes clear that Sade, in staging his apology within the parameters of the law's dictates, keeps a distance from the implications of this commandment unto Christian charity. For Lacan, however, this commandment does not imply a pacified love between men, but rather the absolute hostility that Freud associated with it in *Civilization and Its Discontents*. Sade's extensive apology for crime functions to recoil from this dimension of *méchanceté*: "We believe that Sade is not close enough to his own wickedness to recognize his neighbor in it. A trait which he shares with many, and notably with Freud. For such is indeed the sole motive of the recoil of beings, sometimes forewarned, before the Christian commandment."[23] As evidence of this recoil, Lacan cites Sade's rejection of the death penalty. "For Sade, we see the test of this, crucial in our eyes, in his refusal of the death penalty, which history, if not logic, would suffice to show is one of the corollaries of Charity."[24] Much as Levinas finds that the fulfillment of the law is overdetermined by a relation between the people and the threat of divine violence, Lacan finds that the history and logic of the death penalty is internal to the fulfillment of the law in the love for the neighbor. To oppose the death penalty, as Sade does, amounts to rejecting the facticity of the law, and thus to repressing the autonomy of desire. In other words, desire as such becomes legible only within the horizon of a sovereign violence. Carl Schmitt famously identifies such violence with the contingent possibility of a decision on the exception embodied by the person of the sovereign — the decision to suspend the validity of the entire law in states of emergency. For Lacan, this horizon becomes the "sinuous" line that constitutes the topology of the fantasy.

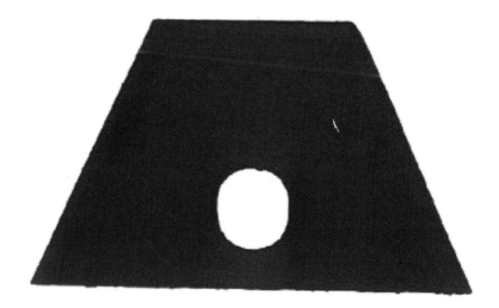

1. Martin Luther King, Jr., *A Testament of Hope: The Essential Speeches and Writings of Martin Luther King, Jr.*, ed. James M. Washington (San Francisco: Harper & Row, 1986), 293.

2. John Rawls, *A Theory of Justice*, rev. ed. (Cambridge: Harvard University Press, Belknap Press, 1970), 3.

3. See Hans Kelsen, *Introduction to the Problems of Legal Theory*, trans. Bonnie Litschewski Paulson and Stanley L. Paulson (Oxford: Clarendon Press, 1992); and Jacques Derrida, "Force of Law: 'The Mystical Foundation of Authority,'" trans. Gil Anidjar, in *Acts of Religion*, ed. Gil Anidjar (New York: Routledge, 2002). For a discussion of Kelsen and Derrida, see Margaret Davies, "Derrida and Law: Legitimate Fictions," in *Jacques Derrida and the Humanities: A Critical Reader*, ed. Tom Cohen (Cambridge: Cambridge University Press, 2001). Throughout this paper, I am further indebted to Juliet Flower MacCannell's reading of Rousseau with Lacan — especially her understanding of the social contract as the "negative law" of universal dispossession. What seems ultimately at stake in such a reading is the determination of whether democracy is essential to the concept of the political, or whether, as Carl Schmitt decided, the concept of the political only emerges with the suspension of the regime of democratic legality. See Juliet Flower MacCannell, *The Hysteric's Guide to the Future Female Subject* (Minneapolis: University of Minnesota Press, 1999). See also Willy Apollon's "Introduction" to *Lacan, Politics, Aesthetics,* ed. Willy Apollon and Richard Feldstein (Albany: State University of New York Press, 1996).

4. The list of attempts to emancipate legal theory from such an entrenchment would also have to include the psychoanalytic teaching of Jacques Lacan, which I will address later in the paper, and Antonio Negri's communist theory of the state. See Antonio Negri, *Insurgencies: Constituent Power and the Modern State,* trans. Maurizia Boscagli (Minneapolis: University of Minnesota Press, 1999); and Michael Hardt and Antonio Negri, *Labor of Dionysus: A Critique of the State-Form* (Minneapolis: University of Minnesota Press, 1994).

5. Kelsen, 26.

6. Derrida's elaboration of the question is incompatible with Kelsen's theory, however, in that, for Derrida, the force of law can never be theorized simply as a "norm," comprehended in terms of a generic attribute. The epistemological aspirations of the theory of law will always encounter insuperable obstacles in the force of law. For Derrida, as for Walter Benjamin, whose text provides the occasion for his intervention, the theory of law must always begin — and perhaps end — with a critique of violence. I will return to this point later, but in connection with a discussion of the presentation of law in psychoanalysis.

7. Rawls, 320.

8. Ibid., 322.

9. Ibid.

10. This aspect of civil disobedience is perhaps not far from the Stoic "contempt" that, at one point in his analysis of Kant and Sade, Lacan levels against the Sadian experience of jouissance. "What [pain] is worth for Sadian experience will be better seen by approaching it through what, in the artifice of the Stoics, would dismantle this experience: contempt...Imagine a revival of Epictetus in Sadian experience: 'See, you broke it,' he says, pointing to his leg. Lowering *jouissance* to the destitution of such an effect where its pursuit stumbles, isn't this to turn it into disgust?" Lacan, "Kant with Sade," trans. James B. Swenson, Jr., *October* 51 (winter 1989): 60. (This translation will be slightly modified throughout.)

11. Arnold Schönberg, *Das Chörwerk*, Sony 2K44571. For an important discussion of the law in Schönberg's opera *Moses und Aron,* see Massimo Caccari, *Icônes de la loi,* French

trans. Marilène Raiola (Paris: Christian Bourgois, 1990). (English translation forthcoming from Stanford University Press.)

12. See Gershom Scholem's essay, "Revelation and Tradition as Religious Categories in Judaism" in *The Messianic Idea in Judaism, And Other Essays on Jewish Spirituality* (New York: Schocken Books, 1971).

13. Emmanuel Levinas, *Nine Talmudic Readings,* trans. and intro. Annette Aronowicz (Bloomington: Indiana University Press, 1990), 40.

14. Immanuel Kant, *Critique of Practical Reason*, ed. and trans. Mary Gregor (Cambridge: Cambridge University Press, 1997), 66. "Fontenelle says: *'I bow before an eminent man, but my spirit does not bow.'* I can add: before a humble common man [*einem niedrigen bürgerlich-gemeinen Mann*] in whom I perceive uprightness of character in a higher degree than I am aware of in myself *my spirit bows*, whether I want it or whether I do not and hold my head ever so high, that he may not overlook my superior position. Why is this? His example holds before me a law that strikes down my self-conceit when I compare it with my conduct, and I see observance of that law and hence its *practicability* proved before me in fact."

15. Ibid., 71.

16. Lacan, *The Seminar of Jacques Lacan, Book II: The Ego in Freud's Theory and in the Technique of Psychoanalysis, 1954-55*, ed. Jacques-Alain Miller, trans. Sylvana Tomaselli (New York: Norton, 1991), 129. (This translation will be slightly modified throughout.)

17. See Lacan, *Écrits* (Paris: Seuil, 1966), 814.

18. Lacan, *The Ego in Freud's Theory*, 128.

19. Ibid., 128, 129.

20. Lacan, "Kant with Sade," 74.

21. Ibid.

22. Benjamin, *Reflections: Essays, Aphorisms, Autobiographical Writings*, ed. and intro. Peter Demetz, trans. Edmund Jephcott (New York: Schocken Books, 1978), 297.

23. Lacan, "Kant with Sade," 74.

24. Ibid.

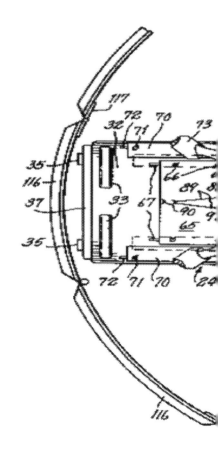

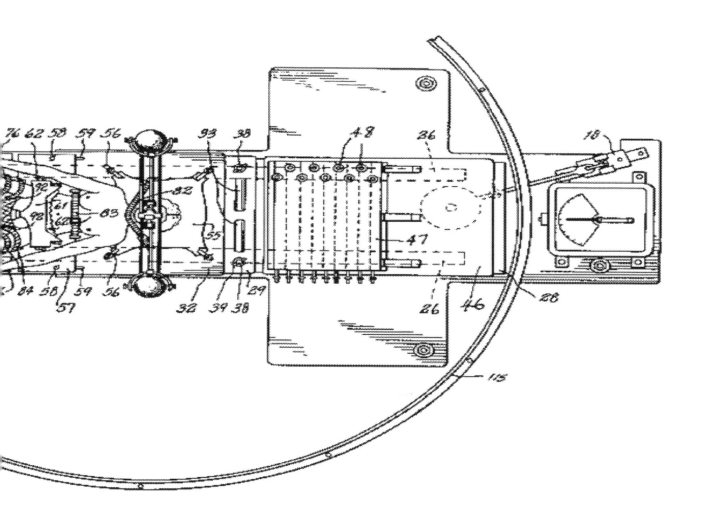

BEING HUMAN: BESTIALITY, ANTHROPOPHAGY, AND LAW

kalpana seshadri-crooks

Every creature that lives and moves shall be food for you; I give you them all, as once I gave you all green plants. But you must not eat the flesh with the life, which is the blood, still in it. And further, for your life-blood I will demand satisfaction; from every animal I will require it, and from a man also I will require satisfaction for the death of his fellow man.

— Genesis 9: 3-5

A man who has sexual intercourse with any beast shall be put to death, and you shall kill the beast. If a woman approaches any animal to have intercourse with it, you shall kill both woman and beast. They shall be put to death; their blood shall be on their own heads.

— Leviticus 20: 15-16

If in spite of this you do not listen to me and still defy me, I will defy you in anger, and I myself will punish you seven times over for your sins. Instead of meat you shall eat your sons and your daughters.

— Leviticus 26: 27-30

The third crimen carnis contra naturam *occurs when the object of the desire is in fact of the opposite sex but is not human. Such is sodomy, or intercourse with animals. This, too, is contrary to the ends of humanity and against our natural instinct. It degrades mankind below the level of animals, for no animal turns in this way from its own species...These vices make us ashamed that we are human beings and, therefore, capable of them, for an animal is incapable of all such* crimina carnis contra naturam.

— Immanuel Kant[1]

The animal is a word, it is an appellation that men have instituted, a name they have given themselves the right and the authority to give to another living creature.

— Jacques Derrida[2]

It is a fundamental observation that Lacanian ethics is grounded in a theory of the subject as the site of a dialectic between the logic of the signifier and the symptom. Insofar as the subject's particularity (its jouissance) and its representability (speech and desire) derive from its positioning with respect to the law, there is an ethics to our conception of this relation between subject and law. By ethics, I mean quite simply a human orientation toward the world, a vigilant reflection of our being in the world and our inescapable engagement with alterity. Such an ethics requires that we go beyond formulaic pronouncements (about never ceding one's desire, and so on) to interrogate the law itself in its function as constitutive of the subject. In other words, how does the law produce human difference? How necessary is such a difference to the functioning of the law? How does the law institute its moral and juridical authority as *identical* to its capacity to produce and secure human difference? Further, how does the law regulate our very conception of non-human alterity, specifically species difference? A psychoanalytic reading of the law positions us at the edge of moral and legal discourse, enabling us to glimpse that which appears at the ontological limit of the human. I propose here to develop a new protocol of reading, one that requires that we think *with* the animal — the animal as and at the limit of human discourses — in order to reinvigorate our engagement with alterity.

With psychoanalysis one can explore the origin of the notion of humanness and the concomitant absolute alterity of non-human creatures. It can also help us clarify the legal transformation of the moral law governing the boundary between human and animal. In its exploration of the moral law, psychoanalysis differs from anthropology and philosophy, two disciplines thought to have privileged access to such law, on at least one significant point: it dwells on prohibition and transgression in a completely non-functionalist way, that is, not as factors of social organization, or the proper or improper workings of reason, but as *symptoms* of what constitutes us as human subjects. Psychoanalysis can no more defend or condemn the moral law than it can offer ethical or sociological prescriptions to cure the fault at the core of human subjectivation. As a discourse on the moral law, psychoanalysis can provide an understanding of the exclusions upon which human difference is founded. Such an understanding would disable our virtually automatic anthropocentrism, the socio-legal celebration of and claims for human sovereignty and transcendence.

Let me clarify at the outset that in approaching the question of the animal through the moral law, I do not mean to harness psychoanalysis for a variant mode of what is now called, within cultural studies, eco-criticism, or to advance the cause of animal rights in a socio-cultural or juridical sense. I believe that the question of the animal is crucial to psychoanalysis because it is at the heart of subject constitution, sexuality, and the law — both moral and juridical. An examination of the exclusions upon which the human is founded may throw light on our contemporary cultural, ethical, and juridical attitudes towards animals. This project, however, is not about the animal *per se*, but about the way in which the law produces its subject as human. While I am interested in how our understanding of the exclusions upon which humanness is founded may rejuvenate our thinking about responsibility to the other and of its autonomy and singularity, my primary concern is the way in which the authority of the law, as a discourse of the constitution of the subject, is predicated on making the animal disappear even as it appears. To think *with* the animal requires discerning the animal as an *iterative device* deployed by the law for self-authorization. This requires that we do not utilize Lacan's theories of subject constitution in a dogmatic way. In fact, this inquiry proceeds from my investment in the profoundly anti-humanist character of Lacanian ethics, whose radical critical edge prevents it from becoming an orthodoxy. No doubt if one were to approach the question of the animal limit by examining Lacan's presuppositions and attitudes about the animal, as Jacques Derrida does, one may be disappointed. As Derrida argues, Lacan's insistent affirmation of the binary human versus animal falls within the purview of received humanist wisdom about animal essences and human transcendence. In what follows, I concur with Derrida's critique of Lacan, but go on to show that if we are interested in the production of the human limit rather than in the animal, Lacan's theories are indispensable.

According to Derrida, Lacan reproduces conventional assumptions about species difference, which are stated as dogmatic truths necessary for the constitution of the human subject. Derrida follows Lacan in *Écrits* closely, tracking his remarks on the animal and species difference to show how his unexamined notions about animals serve to contradict and subvert crucial aspects of his theories. (Derrida coins the term *animot* — a pun on the plural *animaux* and *le mot* for "word" — to point to our way of referring to all animals, the rest of creation, as the signifier that subtends the binary logic.) Because of the specular nature of animal sexuality in Lacan's work on the mirror stage, the animal is confined to the imaginary and distinguished routinely from the human as lacking access to the symbolic — language, law, desire, agency, and the unconscious. According to Derrida, Lacan relies too heavily on a Cartesian economy of the subject whose speech is distinguished as human in that it is a response to the other and not an automatic reaction or a coded fixed correlation (distinctive of the animal-machine) between signs and reality. Derrida writes: "My hesitation concerns only the purity, the rigor, and the indivisibility of the frontier that separates — already with respect to 'us humans' — reaction from response; and as a consequence, especially, the purity, rigor, and indivisibility of the concept of responsibility that ensues."[3] Derrida is skeptical of Lacan's pronouncements regarding response and reaction because such a notion of human agency discounts the impact of the unconscious on human freedom, on the automaticity of responses given the logic of repetition endemic to the unconscious, and the location of ethics and the concept of the human itself in the distinction between reaction and response.

For Derrida, Lacan's discourse on the animal, dependant as it is on Enlightenment humanist certainties regarding the so-called human response, is a form of disavowal. This is most evident in Lacan's discussion of negation and its implication in the logic of pretense and lying. Briefly, Lacan suggests that the form of negation involved in double deception, as in the Jewish joke recounted by Freud ("Why do you tell me that you are going to X in order to have me believe you are going to Y whereas you are indeed going to X?"), is precisely what the animal cannot do. The animal can deceive the hunter or lure its sexual partner; it can make false tracks, but it cannot erase its own tracks. It cannot, in other words, make true tracks appear false. Such an erasure, according to Lacan, would entail the animal becoming a subject of the signifier, which is essentially impossible. Therefore, the animal's existence in the imaginary, where it merely reacts to "vital situations,"[4] also means that it cannot be conditioned by its own word — as in vouching for something or lying — which more or less expels it from time and mortality. The implication here is that the animal lacks the lack that constitutes the human subject. It is a wholly sufficient entity in that it lives in a state that is anterior to good and evil. It is neither a subject of language, nor subjected to language in the manner that the human necessarily must be because of the biological fact of his or her premature birth. Thus, as Derrida points out, the human subject in Lacan is constituted by its lack, which is what distinguishes human from animal.

Another moment of disavowal that Derrida discerns in Lacan pertains to the radical alterity of the Other, which cannot be a fellow subject even if the latter speaks in the place of the Other, the Other as that which goes beyond specular duality. And here Derrida is compelled to ask:

> Must not this place of the Other be ahuman? If this is indeed the case, then the ahuman or at least the figure of some — in a word — *divinanimality*, even if it were to be felt through the human, would be the quasi-transcendental referent, the excluded, foreclosed, disavowed, tamed, and sacrificed foundation of what it founds, namely, the symbolic order, the human order, law, and justice. Is not this necessity performed secretly in Levinas and in Lacan...? That is one of the reasons why it is so difficult to utter a discourse of mastery or of transcendence with regard to the animal and to simultaneously claim to do it in the name of God, in the name of the name of the Father or in the name of the Law. Must not one recognize Father, Law, Animal, and so on, as being, in the final analysis, the same thing — or, rather, indissociable figures of the same Thing?[5]

Derrida is no doubt right in identifying the Other as the place of the ahuman. Indeed, Lacan speaks of the Other as a locus where *it* speaks. As Derrida acknowledges, for Lacan there is no Other of the Other. Lacan suggests in *Encore*, however, that jouissance, insofar as it is in excess of the Other, serves this function.[6] This is the productive moment in Lacan: the Other as ahuman, the jouissance of the Other, and the law that subjects us all — AnimAll — to the moral order. While I sympathize with his project of interrogating the absolute binary between human and animal, Derrida fails to acknowledge the multiplicity — the fungibility even — of the psychoanalytic subject. "Divinanimality" is not disavowed in Lacan; it is, rather, at the heart of Lacan's notion of the moral law.

ANIMOT/ANIMALL

In the Names-of-the-Father seminar, Lacan takes up the institution and origin of the moral law and the paternal metaphor. He focuses on two scenarios: the Freudian myth of the father of the primal horde and the Biblical story of Abraham and Isaac. In both scenarios, Lacan introduces the figure of the animal. The animal appears first in the context of his discussion of Freud's *Totem and Taboo*:

> If the Other is as I say, the place where "it" — *ça* — speaks, it can pose only one kind of problem, that of the subject prior to the question. And Freud intuited this admirably...Mythically, the father — and that is what *mythically* means — can only be an animal.

> The primordial father is the father from before the incest taboo, before the appearance of law, of the structures of marriage and kinship, in a word, of culture. The father is the head of that horde whose satisfaction, in accordance with the animal myth, knows no bounds. That Freud should call him a *totem* takes on its full meaning in the light of the progress brought to the question by the structuralist critique of Lévi-Strauss, which, as you know, brings into relief the classificatory essence of the totem.[7]

For Lacan, though the story of the primal horde explains the origin of the moral law and the structures of kinship, it does not delineate the function of "the paternal metaphor": "We thus see that as a second term what is needed at the level of the father is that function whose definition I believe I developed further in one of my seminars than had ever been done until now — the function of the proper name."[8] The second scenario Lacan takes up is the sacrifice of Isaac as depicted by Caravaggio's famous painting, which offers a supplementary reading of the proper name. There is a relation between these two scenarios, with the second functioning as the supplement to the first.

In the primal horde story, the father, who is an animal, is killed. He is thereupon symbolized by an(other) animal, the totem, that names the tribe. The tribe derives its name from the animal ancestor that has been sacrificed for the sake of the law. According to Freud and Lacan, the law, derived from the horrific murder of the father, is the moral prohibition against incest, or the unrestricted and unregulated sexuality of the horde. What is usually overlooked is that this fundamental law of social organization is itself supported by a complex of other taboos that are ontologically prior. Let us recall Freud:

> The most primitive kind of organization that we actually come across — and one that is in force to this day in certain tribes — consists of bands of males; these bands are composed of members with equal

rights and are subject to the restrictions of the totemic system, including inheritance through the mother. Can this form of organization have developed out of the other one? and if so along what lines?

If we call the celebration of the totem meal to our help, we shall be able to find an answer. One day the brothers who had been driven out came together, killed and devoured their father and so made an end of the patriarchal horde. United, they had the courage to do and succeeded in doing what would have been impossible for them individually. (Some cultural advance, perhaps, command over some new weapon, had given them a sense of superior strength.) Cannibal savages as they were, it goes without saying that they devoured their victim as well as killing him. The violent primal father had doubtless been the feared and envied model of each one of the company of brothers: and in the act of devouring him they accomplished their identification with him, and each one of them acquired a portion of his strength. The totem meal, which is perhaps mankind's earliest festival, would thus be a repetition and a commemoration of this memorable and criminal deed, which was the beginning of so many things — of social organization, of moral restrictions and of religion.[9]

Freud's emphasis here is on the incorporation of the father by the brothers — anthropophagy is primary. This act, according to Freud, is followed by remorse:

A sense of guilt made its appearance, which in this instance coincided with the remorse felt by the whole group. The dead father became stronger than the living one had been — for events took the course we so often see them follow in human affairs to this day...They revoked their deed by forbidding the killing of the totem, the substitute for their father; and they renounced its fruits by resigning their claim to the women who had now been set free. They thus created out of their filial sense of guilt the two fundamental taboos of totemism, which for that very reason inevitably corresponded to the two repressed wishes of the Oedipus complex. Whoever contravened those taboos became guilty of the only two crimes [murder and incest] with which primitive society concerned itself.

The two taboos of totemism with which human morality has its beginning are not on a par psychologically.[10]

Clearly, the prohibition of incest that engenders kinship relations is founded on, even causally related to, the prohibition against murder. For Freud, both prohibitions emerge out of the social contract devised by the brothers, who in order to avoid the fate of the father agree to regulate sexual relations with their clanswomen and guarantee one another's lives. However, if we take seriously Lacan's view that the father of the primal horde was an animal (the horde itself a group of ahuman animals), distinguished by his enjoyment, his unrestricted sexual freedom, something more than inexplicable guilt and the pragmatism of the social contract comes into view — the problem of the subject prior to the question. We must read the murder of the father as the moment not only of the institution of the prohibitions against murder and incest, but of the very notion of the human, of the separation between human and animal, and of their interrelation.

The prohibition on murder, from which the sexual taboos and kinship structures derive, now takes on an additional meaning. It must also be the moment when murder itself is distinguished from other forms of killing as a specific transgression against human life and law.[11] In other words, the newly instituted concept of murder organizes acts of killing according to the object: those that can be killed (sanctioned slaughter) and those that cannot be killed (murder). The former group is comprised of the animal, in its difference from the human, as food or as sacrificial object. There is thus a prohibition not only against killing humans, but also against eating them. Freud is quite right to designate the totem meal as the key to the origin of the moral law, but what Lacan leads us to note in addition is the relation between murder and food, which founds species difference, perhaps on a relation of specular likeness and difference.

How then does species difference, emerging as it does out of these newly instituted prohibitions against murder and anthropophagy, impact sexual relations? Does it have any bearing on the incest taboo and kinship relations? Lacan makes the answer clear. If the father of the horde was an animal, then surely the time before the law is also the *anachronistic* scenario of bestiality: sex before differentiation. Introducing the question of the subject prior to the question — species difference — enables us to see that the moral prohibitions against murder and incest are shadowed by prohibitions against cannibalism and bestiality. In fact, the former prohibitions cannot possibly function without the latter set of ancillary taboos. The totem memorializes the time before the law, before the moral prohibitions against incest and murder, before species difference. The moral law is supported in a sense by two supplementary laws that are ontologically necessary: the prohibitions on bestiality and anthropophagy. Lacan seems to suggest that the Freudian myth of the primal horde is also the myth of the constitution of the cannibal and the bestialist — the transgressors of the law before the law. This submerged matrix of prohibitions comes more sharply into view when we consider that one of the functions of the moral law is to establish a mutually exclusive opposition between those we use for food and those we use for sex (that is, we may not have sex with the food object or turn our sexual object into food). In *The Savage Mind*, Claude Lévi-Strauss, though not on the track of species difference, acknowledges the "profound analogy which people throughout the world seem to find between copulation and eating."[12] He provides several examples of languages, including French, which use the same word to denote both activities; interestingly, he insists that it is hopeless "to attempt to establish a relation of priority between nutritional prohibitions and rules of exogamy. The connection between them is not causal but metaphorical."[13] Lévi-Strauss explains this "universal" association by suggesting that "the lowest common denominator of the union of the sexes and the union of eater and eaten is that they both effect a *conjunction by complementarity*."[14] Undoubtedly, our contemporary association of food and sex functions on the analogy of incorporation (if not heterosexist complementarity), but the issue of species difference discloses the inherent practical connection between food and sex.[15] It is not so much that food prohibitions are prior in some way, but that the simultaneity of the prohibitions against anthropophagy and bestiality

effectively disarticulates sex from food, leaving us with little but the meaty metaphor of inges-
tion and union. The extraordinary depth of the interrelation of these prohibitions is perhaps
most evident in our relations with the family pet, which, like one's kin, may not be regarded as
food or sex object.[16]

Lacan's assertion that the primal father must have been an animal, insofar as the so-called
animal is characterized by a satisfaction that knows no bounds, also raises the question of the
animal as such as a mythic creature, a grammatical function that must be posited to grasp the
organization of (sexual) meaning.[17] I am alluding here to the graph of sexual difference that Lacan
develops in *Encore*.[18] We can read the first set of formulae as mapping the structure of the primal
horde myth and the relation of all subjects to castration. In fact, given the implications of thinking
through the primal father as an animal for the institution and significance of the moral law, the
question of the existence of the animal as an ontic category becomes impossible. From an angle of
approach completely different from Derrida's, Lacan leads us to ask: does the animal exist?

If the fantasy of the uncastrated animal/father makes a genealogy of the moral law possible, it
does not fully account for the linguistic function of the proper name, of the Name-of-the-Father.
After his brief exposition of the top half of the graph of sexual difference, Lacan goes on to speak
about the symbols below: "Underneath, beneath the line going across where it intersects with
the vertical division of what is incorrectly called humanity, inasmuch as it can be divided up into
sexual identifications, you have a rough lay out of what goes on."[19] I suggest we read this am-
biguous sentence as meaning that the horizontal division marks the split between (what is
incorrectly called) humanity and ahumanity, as well as the division within humanity along lines
of sexual difference.

For Lacan, the attribution of totality to the father as the place of unmitigated jouissance cannot
account for the *functionality* of the Other as barred or lacking, for the state of language as always
already compensatory, entailing the necessity of the proper name, the ensuing necessary difference between desire and jouissance required for the functioning of the proper name (as in the
Oedipal scenario) and the formation of the superego. There is a perceived need to locate the
logos in its function not only as constitutive of the subject, but also of the order of being in
relation to the moral law. In the Names-of-the-Father seminar, Lacan says:

> It is clear that, in his myth, Freud finds a singular balance, a kind of co-conformity — if I may be
> allowed to thus double my prefixes — of Law and desire, stemming from the fact that both are born
> together, joined and necessitated by each other in the law of incest and what? — the supposition of the
> pure erotic bliss of the father viewed as primordial.

> Except, if that is alleged to give us the formation of desire in the child, ought we not — I have insisted
> on this at length for years — to pose the question of knowing why all this yields neuroses?[20]

To grasp the condition of the subject as lacking, caught up in an economy of desire and anxiety, one requires a supplementary genealogy, another narrative of the law. And this time, it is not the primordial father's bliss, veiled and inscrutable, but his demand that is significant. For Lacan, it is the category of perversion that discloses most clearly the desire of the Other, here interpreted as Eternal God or supreme being. What becomes salient in this particular problematic is God's desire (as opposed to his jouissance) "as interested in the order of the world" and neurosis (perverse or normal desire) as the "flight from the term of the father's desire."[21] It is in order to delineate this complex of relations that Lacan turns to the Biblical story of Abraham and Isaac. Interestingly, he particularizes this story as distinctly Judeo-Christian, one that helps distinguish this tradition from all other mystical traditions by its hook into the eye of God's demand to man, of his desire in the world. This emphasis on the subject's relation to the desire of the Other introduces an added juridical dimension to our understanding of the status of the animal in psychoanalysis and the moral law.

Lacan offers a complex reading of Abraham's sacrifice, or the *Akedah* (the binding) as it is known in the Jewish tradition, as the intervention of the function of the signifier: as the mark of lack (prohibition of jouissance) and of difference and signification (naming). Two aspects of this God are significant: first, he is the one whose name is ineffable, whose name we are forbidden to pronounce; second, he is indicated by the affect of anxiety. Several names come into play here: *Shem* (the Forbidden Name), *Elohim* (the Almighty), and *El Shadday* (the Guardian of the Doors of Israel).[22] It is in the name of *El Shadday* that the angel speaks and restrains Abraham's hand as he is about to sacrifice his son. The unutterable signifier of God prohibits Abraham from serving God's jouissance. This is the key point of the *Akedah* according to Lacan: it marks the cut between God's jouissance and his desire. "Here may be marked the knife blade separating God's bliss from what in that tradition is presented as his desire."[23] The logic of substitution that is then introduced engenders the play of difference — metaphor (the ram) and metonymy (the foreskin). Lacan insists that the ram is "not a metaphor of the father at the level of phobia." In other words, the ram is not what he refers to in *Encore* as *la bêtise*, the nonsense that characterizes animal phobia. He introduces the term *Shofar* (the ram's horn), which refers to the hollow sounding horn used to herald freedom and assemble the community. In the Jewish tradition, it is a reminder of the sacrifice of Abraham. The ram that rushes onto the scene of sacrifice, Lacan suggests, is the "primeval ram." It was present during the seven days of creation and is therefore originary — an *Elohim*, an "ancestor of the race of Sem, he who links Abraham, through a rather short path, to origins." The ram is Abraham's "eponymous ancestor, the God of his race"; it is the material manifestation of Abraham's "biological origin" for "[t]he thing whose downfall it is a matter of provoking is biological origin."[24]

We can perhaps understand this "provocation," in which the eponymous ancestor is surrendered as origin, by way of Derrida's commentary on Adam's naming of the animals in Genesis.

Working with two French translations of Genesis, Derrida remarks on the command issued by God to man (in another translation, man and woman) to command the animals, and then to name them: "he has created man in his likeness *so that* man will *subject, tame, dominate, train,* or *domesticate* the animals born before him and assert his authority over them…However, everything seems to happen as though God still wanted to oversee, keep vigil, maintain his right of inspection over the names that were about to echo out and by means of which Ish [Adam], Ish all alone, Ish still without woman, was going to get the upper hand with respect to the animals." [25] Derrida makes two significant points: first, Adam names "these living things that came into the world before him but were named after him"; second, this God who summons the animals to Adam marks "an all powerful God *and* the finitude of a God who doesn't know what is going to happen to him with language. And with names. In short, God doesn't yet know what he really wants; this is the finitude of a God who doesn't know what he wants with respect to the animal." [26] For Derrida, Adam's naming of the animals, his being *after* the animals — in the sense of both coming after their birth, and after them as in capture or domination — is not in time but is the genesis of time. Thus God's "exposure to surprise, to the event of what is going to occur between man and animal, [is] this time before time" itself. [27] But there is another sense in which man is after the animal: he names himself after the animal that he names. The totem animal is not *yet* the moment of the logos. It is an entirely immanent signifier of man's origins. It is surely this *secular* relation between human and animal that is addressed and annulled through the story of Abraham and Isaac.

In the "later" scenario of the Abrahamic sacrifice, God revokes the names that man has given to his creatures and to himself. The substitution of the ram, his ancestor, for Isaac, his progeny, can be understood as accomplishing two things. First, Abraham distinguishes God's desire from his jouissance thereby preserving the place of the Other as barred (what Derrida terms his "finitude") — lacking, incomplete, yet paradoxically all-powerful in its insatiability. Second, the totemic ancestor is now subordinated to the name of God as ineffable. In other words, the (once autonomous) animal, the source of the name and origin of the community, is sacrificed to the name of the father, thus orienting man to the transcendental. Henceforth, the community will be assembled through the voice of the ram, the *Shofar*, in the name of God and his desire. The law of circumcision — the little piece of flesh sliced off — marks God's desire towards his chosen people. Between the metaphor of the *Shofar* and the metonym of the foreskin, God institutes an order, a moral order that subjects all — AnimAll — to his law. God institutes the difference between human and animal by imposing his law of hierarchy upon all creation: the logos as a great disciplinary apparatus disclosing its hierarchical function even as it subjects all — human and animal — to a univocal and calibrated law. In other words, the intervention of the logos as God's desire expressed through the name fixes, once and for all, an ethico-juridical imperative, the difference between human and animal by imposing what was once called "The Great Chain of Being."[28]

The sovereignty of God, the subordination or subjection of the animal ancestor to the Other, has paradoxical consequences for species difference. There is an intensification of the line separating human and animal, even as there is an increased anthropomorphization of the animal. This paradox is demonstrably enshrined in Western juridical discourse through the ages, and founds the unacknowledged discursive conditions of possibility for our contemporary debates about animal rights and species difference.

(ANIM)ALL ARE SUBJECT TO THE LAW

Because we understand the legal system as a quintessentially human institution, it is not surprising that contemporary law does not hold animals responsible for their actions. While the law addresses animals either to protect them from extinction and wanton cruelty, or to prevent them from being used as instruments of legal violation against other humans, this has not always been the case. A historical exploration of the law in relation to animals discloses an altogether forgotten archive. In his *The Criminal Prosecution and Capital Punishment of Animals*, E. P. Evans shows that contrary to modern practice, it was routine in many parts of Europe to prosecute animals in courts of law and to stage punishments as spectacles if they were convicted of criminal wrongdoing. Evans' book is an exhaustive discussion of the trials — ecclesiastical and juridical — of various largely domestic animals and insects that caused injury to human beings. In a tone of incredulity bordering on contempt, he cites numerous cases, beginning with one recorded by the distinguished sixteenth-century French jurist Bartholomew Chassenée, who defended (as he did in several cases of animals charged with criminal behavior) a group of rats being sued for the wanton destruction of a barley crop.[29] For Evans, the anthropomorphization evident in the treatment of so-called criminal animals is suggestive of the kind of superstition that led to the persecution of witches. Arguing against nineteenth-century scholar Léon Ménébrea, who suggested that such trials should be interpreted as noble evidence of the respect for creation and all creatures in Western civil society, Evans writes:

> So far from originating in a delicate and sensitive sense of justice, it was...the outcome of an extremely crude, obtuse, and barbaric sense of justice. It was the product of a social state, in which dense ignorance was governed by brute force, and is not to be considered as a reaction and protest against club-law, which it really tended to foster by making a travesty of the administration of justice and thus turning it into ridicule. It was also in the interest of ecclesiastical dignities to keep up this parody and perversion of a sacred and fundamental institute of civil society, since it strengthened their influence and extended their authority by subjecting even the caterpillar and the canker-worm to their dominion and control.[30]

Despite the richness and peculiarity of the archival material Evans exhumes, his work is marked by sweeping generalizations, and displays a marked impatience for making distinctions across cultures, histories, and meanings. Evans' attitude is echoed much later by legal philosopher Hans Kelsen in his classic work *General Theory of Law and State*. Kelsen notes that "[i]n primitive law, animals, and even plants and other inanimate objects are often treated in the same way as human beings and are, in particular, punished. However, this must be seen in its connection with the animism of primitive man. He considers animals, plants, and inanimate objects as endowed with a 'soul,' inasmuch as he attributes human, and sometimes even superhuman, mental facilities to them. The fundamental difference between human and other beings, which is part of the outlook of civilized man, does not exist for primitive man."[31]

For a more nuanced approach to this archive, it is necessary to turn to J. J. Finkelstein, whose brilliant monograph, *The Ox That Gored*, also addresses the criminal prosecution of animals. Finkelstein cites the above passage from Kelsen as typical of assumptions made by social theorists ignorant of the historical and unconscious bases of their own laws. As Finkelstein writes, "my purpose here is not to take issue with Kelsen or with others whose approach to legal institutions is much in the same vein. Rather, I wish to stress here...how the failure to become conscious of one's unconscious premises, and to subject them to the most searching scrutiny, effectively undermines the grandest schemes."[32] Finkelstein's rather surprising research, based on a comparative study of Biblical and Mesopotamian law regarding accidental human death caused by animals, offers an altogether more thoughtful and philosophically satisfying explanation than do either Evans or Kelsen. He suggests that "[s]ocieties of non-Western derivation and primitive peoples *did not and do not* attribute 'human' will or 'human' personality to animals or things, and *never* have tried them or punished them as they did human offenders. The notion that trials and punishments of irrational creatures and of inanimate things are a valid legal procedure occurs *uniquely* in Western society."[33] Finkelstein sifts through the historical evidence of the trial and punishment of domestic animals in medieval and Enlightenment Europe, distinguishing between the mock trials (magico-ritual acts) conducted by the church to rid society of a menace and the authentic juridical trials of offending animals. The former scenario, in which weevils or rodents are excommunicated or anathematized, mimics legal processes to solicit the aid of supernatural powers to resolve a problem. In the latter, the question is one of "a human verdict and a social action" directed at a domestic animal that is ostensibly in violation of the law.[34] The earliest case, recorded in 1266, is the trial of a pig.[35]

While Finkelstein is attentive to geographical and rhetorical differences in the trial and punishment of animals, in his view the trials were not much different from morality plays that offered simple lessons in good conduct. He insists that, rather than revealing a residue of

Execution of a Sow in front of the Church at Falaise

"primitive mentality," as propounded by Evans and Kelsen, for example, such trials were attempts, with the increased influence of Canon Law, to bring society into greater conformity with Biblical prescriptions and principles of classification.[36] Finkelstein writes:

> It is, however, vital for us to perceive that the medieval rationale for the execution of homicidal domestic animals is not the consequence of any confusion in Western thinking about the capacity for will or intention in animals or in inanimate things, even though there have been times, as we have seen, when such ideas did become manifest on the folk level. On the whole, however, the reverse is true: there is an unbridgeable gulf between mankind and the rest of creation, and there is beyond that an acute sensitivity towards boundary breaching between kinds within the world of living things. This is indeed the key to this strange and apparently irrational practice. Animals that have killed persons were to be extirpated because the very fact of their having done so disturbed the cosmological environment in a way that could not be tolerated: the act appeared to negate the *hierarchically* differentiated order of creation by which man was granted sovereignty in the physical world.[37]

Finkelstein's observation about the significance of these animal trials as part of a cosmological worldview resonates with Lacan's discussion of the moral law as instituted by the intervention of the logos and the Name-of-the-Father. It stands to "reason" that in a universe where God's dominion is manifested by the Great Chain of Being, an ox that gores or a pig that molests threatens the entire order.

The same rationale, and perhaps something more, is also at work in the numerous trials and executions of humans and animals for engaging in buggery or bestiality (severely proscribed in

Exod. 22:19 and Lev. 20:13-16). According to Evans, such acts were "uniformly punished by putting to death both parties implicated, and usually by burning them alive."[38] The severity of the punishment of both partners — flaying, burning alive, scattering of ashes — attests to the great anxiety and perceived threat associated with such crimes. Examples abound: in 1466, a man and a sow were burned in Corbeil by order of the parliament of Paris; in 1546, the same court ordered a man and cow hanged and burned; in 1609, in Niederrad a man and a mare were executed and buried in a carrion-pit; in 1606, a man and a bitch were burned in Chartres; in 1662, in New England one Mr. Potter was forced to witness the hanging of his partners in crime before he was himself executed.[39] In this litany of crimes and horrific punishments, one trial stands out as remarkable: that of Jacques Ferron, who was caught in the act with a she-ass in Vanvres in 1750. After much deliberation, the court acquitted the donkey, reasoning that she was a victim of the crime, not a willing sexual partner. Having known her for several years, the parish priest and the community of Vanvres vouched that the ass was a virtuous and well-behaved creature. In a signed certificate, the community asserted that "'they were willing to bear witness that she is in word and deed and in all her habits of life a most honest creature.'"[40] Ferron, however, was executed, thus containing a threat that surely must have been perceived as more than rebellion against the cosmic order.

It is obvious that bestiality threatens the very foundations of the moral law as the demarcation of species categories and kinship relations. Historian Jonas Liliequist suggests that though bestiality became a capital offense in Sweden in the thirteenth century, animal prosecutions reached their peak in the seventeenth and eighteenth centuries when bestiality accounted for 25-35 per cent of all capital punishments. Liliequist notes that in the formulation of the questions at such trials, "an implicit analogy was set up between bestiality and cannibalism: making love to a beast is like eating human flesh. This correspondence reveals an essential meaning of bestiality, as it implies not only moral corruption and foolishness but a defilement in the most physical sense. This is also the connotation of the word *abominable* used in the Pentateuch and in legal texts."[41] The offending animal was invariably ostracized and publicly executed along with its human lover to rid society of the abomination. Finkelstein suggests that bestiality was punished as severely and dramatically as it was because the act was an offense against divine creation by violating the hierarchical order of the universe that places man above all other creatures, upsetting the fundamental principle of creation as the separation and ordering of species and their boundaries. However, I argue that, given the extreme and severe measures against the offenders, what is threatened is not just the abstract order of creation, the divine decree "that propagation shall be 'each after its own kind.'"[42] Rather, bestiality threatens more specifically the one boundary separating human and animal, a boundary that has been very jealously guarded by theologians, philosophers, and lawmakers: speech and discourse as the preserve of man. Bestiality, the fantasmatic scenario of what a human being may do, the positions he or she may assume with respect to quadrupeds, threatens not so much the degradation of man to the level of animal but the opposite: it threatens to bring the animal into discourse, as an agent and a subject. The animal's cries, moans, and grunts in the act of coition are an address to the human partner. Here in the buggery stable, the animal does not merely react as a Cartesian animal-machine, it *responds*. The laws against bestiality disclose above all the pornographic foundation of the moral law itself. And, of course, the pornography of the law is also its own self-authorization.

HUMANIMALISM

What do we make of the fact that in contemporary legal discourse, bestiality as a perversion or a legal infraction seems almost totally absent? Culturally, it seems archaic, outmoded, at best a practice associated with the rural farmhand. Judging from the fact that it is rarely mentioned in the study of sexuality, it seems to have been eclipsed by other (more sophisticated) sexual perversions. According to the Animal Sexual Abuse Information and Resource Site (ASAIRS), however, bestiality is an all-too-popular form of abuse.[43] Along with the Humane Society of the United States (HSUS), it aims to enforce existing laws that criminalize bestiality, and also supports wider legislative measures targeting so-called zoophiles. They hold that bestiality, even when the human partner professes to love his dog or horse or cow, can never be anything but abuse, as the animal is always physically injured and often killed in the process. In spite of their efforts, only roughly half of the United States consider bestiality a criminal act.[44]

It is significant that the history of animal prosecutions has been deliberately excised from official historical narratives; a similar deafening silence has surrounded bestiality in contemporary discourse. I would suggest that what we have seen over time is a discursive shift from enacting laws against the criminal animal and the inter-species practice of bestiality, to the expunging of the non-human from legal discourse. In a reversal of the Foucauldian scenario, in which power and discourse produce sexuality, what we have now is an alliance between silence and power, the progressive muting and desexualization of the animal.

Within this context, the struggle of animal rights activists, for example, lobbying in cases of wrongful death of companion animals for recognition of emotional distress rather than mere market value of the animal, actually enforces species difference. The human is even more human for his or her sensitivity to animals, and the animal is even more animal because it is the mute and pathetic victim of superior human cruelty. The human is compensated for his or her delicate sensitivity and consequent suffering from loss, whereas the animal is not recognized as having innate rights to life or dignity. In fact, we could say that the ethics of the animal rights movement is founded on a profound human narcissism: because animals are like us and can feel and suffer, they must be granted such and such. Paradoxically, such rights, even as they seek to extend the logic of human rights to non-humans, can only do so on the basis of rigidifying the line separating the species. Undeniably, the animal must be rendered completely mute and passive in relation to humans in order to be accorded the protections (against human violence) that rights promise. The main affect generated by such discourse — the images used and the descriptive language regarding the helplessness and vulnerability of the animal — is pathos. The sad-eyed animal gazing out at us from the animal rights poster solicits our compassion, but it does so silently. In a sense, there is continuity between older laws punishing bestiality and our more contemporary silence towards the practice: both practices produce the animal as voiceless. A thorough and radical anti-speciesism will require an axiology of human rights itself, a turn toward a new humanimalism. Psychoanalysis uncovers the deep logic of the constitutive structures of the human subject necessary for such a revaluation. If species difference, the concept of the animal, is constitutive of the human, and if his or her access to the moral law and the paternal function is determined by this binary opposition, the ethical questions that follow cannot be merely critical philosophical. They will entail an intervention at the level of the fundamental fantasy of being human.

1. Immanuel Kant, *Lectures on Ethics*, trans. Louis Infield (New York: Harper & Row, 1963), 170-171.

2. Jacques Derrida "The Animal That Therefore I Am (More to Follow)," trans. David Wills, *Critical Inquiry* 28 (winter 2002), 392.

3. Derrida, "And Say the Animal Responded?" trans. David Wills, in *Zoontologies: The Question of the Animal*, ed. Cary Wolfe (Minneapolis: University of Minnesota Press, 2003), 127. I thank Cary Wolfe for making this essay available to me before its publication.

4. Ibid., 131.

5. Ibid., 134.

6. See Jacques Lacan, *The Seminar of Jacques Lacan, Book XX: Encore: On Feminine Sexuality, The Limits of Love and Knowledge, 1972-1973*, ed. Jacques-Alain Miller, trans. Bruce Fink (New York: Norton, 1998), esp. 1-13.

7. Lacan, "Introduction to the Names-of-the-Father Seminar," in *Television/A Challenge to the Psychoanalytic Establishment*, ed. Joan Copjec, trans. Denis Hollier, Rosalind Krauss, and Annette Michelson (New York: Norton, 1990), 88.

8. Ibid.

9. Sigmund Freud, *Totem and Taboo*, in *The Standard Edition of the Complete Psychological Works of Sigmund Freud*, ed. and trans. James Strachey et al. (London: Hogarth Press, 1953-1974), 13:141-142.

10. Ibid., 143-144.

11. This is a point that Derrida does not recognize when he writes apropos the general singular of "the animal": "The confusion of all nonhuman living creatures within the general and common category of the animal is not simply a sin against rigorous thinking, vigilance, lucidity, or empirical authority; it is also a crime. Not a crime against animality precisely, but a crime of the first order against the animals, against animals. Do we agree to presume that every murder, every transgression of the commandment 'Thou shalt not kill' concerns only man...and that in sum there are only crimes 'against humanity'?" "The Animal That Therefore I Am," 416.

12. Claude Lévi-Strauss, *The Savage Mind* (Chicago: University of Chicago Press, 1966), 105. See also his *Totemism*, trans. Rodney Needham (Boston: Beacon Press, 1963).

13. Lévi-Strauss, *The Savage Mind*, 105.

14. Ibid., 105-106.

15. For an amusing and erudite study of the metaphor of incorporation in Western culture, see Maggie Kilgour's *From Communion to Cannibalism: An Anatomy of Metaphors of Incorporation* (Princeton: Princeton University Press, 1990). See also C. J. Rawson, "Cannibalism and Fiction," parts 1 and 2, *Genre* 11 (spring 1977-1978): 667-711 and 227-313 respectively.

16. Midas Dekkers' *Dearest Pet: On Bestiality* (London: Verso, 1994) is an engaging romp through the ages on the representation of bestiality. The book gained notoriety after Peter Singer's endorsement of the book (and implicitly of bestiality itself) in a review entitled "Heavy Petting," http://www.nerve.com/Opinions/Singer/heavyPetting/main.asp.

17. In *Encore*, Lacan writes the (animal) father before the moral law, prior to castration as $\exists X \, \Phi X$: there is One that is not subject to the paternal metaphor. This is a necessary presupposition for the organization of sexual difference (78).

18. Lacan's formula for sexual difference using symbolic logic reads roughly as follows: on the male side, "There is one that is not subject to the phallic function; All are subject to the phallic function"; on the female side, "There is not one that is not subject to the phallic function; Not all are subject to the phallic function."

19. Quoted in Lacan, *Feminine Sexuality*, ed. Juliet Mitchell and Jacqueline Rose, trans. Jacqueline Rose (New York: Norton, 1985), 150. Fink translates this sentence in *Encore* as follows: "Underneath — that is, below the horizontal bar where the vertical bar (*division*) is crossed over, that division of what is improperly called humanity is divided up into sexual identifications — you have a scanded indication of what is in question" (80).

20. Lacan, "Names-of-the-Father," 89.

21. Ibid.

22. D'vorah, *Hebrew Glossary*, <http://www.headcoverings-by-devorah.com/HebglossA.html> (1 April 2003).

23. Lacan, "Names-of-the-Father," 94.

24. Ibid.

25. Derrida, "The Animal That Therefore I Am," 386.

26. Ibid.

27. Ibid., 387.

28. For an intellectual history of the concept, see Arthur O. Lovejoy, *The Great Chain of Being: A Study of the History of an Idea* (Cambridge: Harvard University Press, 1936).

29. E. P. Evans, *The Criminal Prosecution and Capital Punishment of Animals* (1906; rpt. New Jersey: Lawbook Exchange, 1998), 18.

30. Ibid., 41.

31. Hans Kelsen, *General Theory of Law and State*, trans. Anders Wedberg (New York: Russell & Russell, 1961), 3-4.

32. J. J. Finkelstein, *The Ox That Gored*, Transactions of the American Philosophical Society, n.s., 71, pt. 2 (Philadelphia, 1981), 49.

33. Ibid., 64.

34. Ibid., 66.

35. Pigs were rather popular victims of the law in general. In *Dearest Pet*, Dekkers cites a 1394 case of a pig in Mortaigne that was tried and sentenced to death by hanging for having committed the sacrilege of eating a blessed host. Finkelstein refers to another trial (1386) of a sow accused of mangling an infant to death. Upon conviction, it was paraded in men's clothing (no discussion here of cross-dressing) and solemnly executed by the public hangman, its body mangled afterward. Scores of other such trials were recorded almost through to the end of the eighteenth century.

36. Finkelstein, 68-69.

37. Ibid., 73.

38. Evans, 147.

39. Ibid., 148-149.

40. Ibid., 150.

41. Jonas Liliequist, "Peasants against Nature: Crossing the Boundaries between Man and Animal in Seventeenth- and Eighteenth-Century Sweden" in *Forbidden History: The State, Society, and the Regulation of Sexuality in Modern Europe*, ed. John C. Fout (Chicago: University of Chicago Press, 1992), 68.

42. Finkelstein, 71.

43. *ASAIRS*, 27 July 2002, <http://www.asairs.com/main_index.htm> (1 April 2003).

44. According to the HSUS, at present only twenty-four states in the U.S. have laws against bestiality on the books. It is considered a felony in five states, and a misdemeanor in the remaining nineteen. However, Richard A. Posner and Katharine B. Silbaugh claim that bestiality is a felony in seventeen states, including Washington D.C., and a misdemeanor in twelve, whereas twenty-two states have no relevant statutes. See *A Guide to America's Sex Laws* (Chicago: University of Chicago Press, 1996), 207-212.

THE LURE OF ANTIGONE:
APORIAS OF AN ETHICS OF THE POLITICAL
yannis stavrakakis

In examining the centrality of the law in Lacanian theory one is led, sooner or later, to *The Ethics of Psychoanalysis*. Here the law is firmly situated within a conceptual constellation of other crucial concepts such as the Thing, jouissance, and sublimation. Furthermore, it is here, already in the first pages of the seminar, that Lacan points to the ever-present association between morality, law, and ethics: "Moral experience as such, that is to say, the reference to sanctions, puts man in a certain relation to his own action that concerns not only an articulated law but also a direction, a trajectory, in a word, a good that he appeals to, thereby engendering an ideal of conduct. All that, too, properly speaking constitutes the dimension of ethics and is situated beyond the notion of command."[1] Following this trajectory, I will discuss some aspects of the ethics of psychoanalysis. The reader, however, should not expect a detailed treatise or a systematic exposition of Lacanian ethics; my aim is much more modest: to articulate a set of aporias in relation to a specific type of appropriation of Lacanian ethics in the service of a politics of radical social transformation.

My main focus will be an article by Slavoj Žižek published in *Umbr(a)* in 1998.[2] In this essay, a reply to Judith Butler's criticism of Lacan, Žižek's argument revolves around the radical character of Lacanian ethics and aims at demonstrating its revolutionary political potential: what is at stake in Žižek's argument is not only the possibility of resisting, but also of undermining or displacing the existing socio-symbolic network, of radically transforming a given power structure. Žižek distinguishes between an imaginary form of resistance, a "false transgression" that ultimately serves to maintain and reproduce the law, and "the effective symbolic rearticulation *via* the intervention of the real of an *act*."[3] This notion of the act thus functions as the nodal point of this syntagm and of Žižek's position in general.

The act is a concept often invoked by Lacan — notice for example the title of his seminar *L'acte psychoanalytique*.[4] It is also central to his

Ethics seminar where Lacan addresses Antigone's act, which pushes to the limit "the realization of something that might be called the pure and simple desire of death as such" since Antigone "incarnates that desire."[5] In his reading of Lacan, Žižek focuses on the death drive as "the elementary form of the *ethical act*,"[6] and on the heroic example — the model — of Antigone, arguing that she "effectively puts at risk her entire social existence, defying the socio-symbolic power of the city embodied in the rule of Creon, thereby 'falling into some kind of death' — i.e., sustaining symbolic death, the exclusion from the socio-symbolic space."[7] In Žižek's reading, there is no ethical act proper without the "risk" of a "momentary" suspension of the big Other. Furthermore, only such a "radical *act*" can engender "a thorough reconfiguration of the entire field which redefines the very conditions of socially sustained performativity."[8] This is, then, where the political significance of Antigone's act lies: "Lacan's wager is that even and also in politics, it *is* possible to accomplish a more radical gesture of 'traversing' the very fundamental fantasy. Only such gestures which disturb this fantasmatic kernel are authentic *acts*."[9] It is also here that Žižek locates a major difference between a deconstructionist ethics of finitude and a Lacanian ethics. In the first case, faced with a constitutive lack, the only ethical option is heroically to assume it: "the corollary of this ethics, of course, is that the ultimate source of totalitarian and other catastrophes is man's presumption that he can overcome this condition of finitude, lack and displacement, and 'act like God,' in a total transparency, surpassing his constitutive division."[10] In contrast, Žižek's Lacanian answer is that "absolute/unconditional acts do occur" and that "the true source of evil is not a finite mortal man who acts like God, but a man who disavows that divine miracles occur and reduces himself to just another finite mortal being."[11]

However appealing this passionate promise of miraculous change may be, particularly in an era of cynical apathy and pessimism, Žižek's argument raises a number of theoretical and political questions. In what follows, I will attempt to highlight some of the tensions inherent in his argument in order to help clarify the Lacanian ethical position and its implications for contemporary transformative politics. There are at least two important issues in trying to evaluate this position: the first is related to Žižek's particular reading of Antigone; the second concerns the general value for Lacanian theory and for politics of what Simon Critchley has described as the "tragic-heroic paradigm."[12]

I.

First of all, Žižek's discussion of Antigone ignores or downplays important aspects of the tragedy itself and Lacan's commentary. In a nutshell: Can Antigone really be presented as a model for progressive ethico-political action? According to Žižek, such an example can be offered only only by someone who "risks" an encounter with death in order to "momentarily" suspend the symbolic/legal network and effect a shift in the existing power structure. Does Antigone fulfill these criteria?

Even a cursory glance at Sophocles' text and Lacan's commentary seems to point to the opposite. Antigone does not merely risk an encounter with symbolic death and a momentary suspension of the laws of the city. In opposing the laws of the city, Creon's ethics of the good(s), she incarnates a pure desire, she achieves an *autonomy* so radical that it can only be associated with real death. In the words of the chorus, "a law to yourself, alone, no mortal like you, ever, you go down to the halls of Death alive and breathing."[13] According to Lacan, Antigone's position is the following: "I am dead and I desire death."[14] In that sense, hers was never a case of risk or suspension. Risk entails a minimum of strategic or pragmatic calculation, which is something alien to Antigone's pure desire. Suspension presupposes a before and an after, but for Antigone there is no after. It is important to distinguish between the two deaths — symbolic and real/actual death — but we should not forget that Antigone opts for both. In that sense, this was never a case of an act effecting a displacement of the status quo. Antigone knows her fate from the beginning — she is involved in a game whose outcome is known in advance — a detail that does not escape Lacan's attention: in almost all of the seven tragedies of Sophocles, "there isn't even the suggestion of a peripetia. Everything is there from the beginning; the trajectories that are set in motion have only to come crashing down one on top of the other as best they can." Moreover, as Lacan points out, "tragic heroes are always isolated, they are always beyond established limits, always in an exposed position and, as a result, separated in one way or another from the structure."[15] Such a position can, of course, function as a radical critique of social structure as such; it is difficult to see, however, how the "inhuman" position of Antigone could point to an alternative formulation of the socio-political structure. The "suicidal heroic ethics" implicit in Lacan's reading of Antigone implies a total neglect of the socio-political world; as Žižek suggests in an earlier text, the motto of such an ethics could only be *"fiat desiderium, pereat mundus."*[16] Antigone's intransigence, her deadly passion, may thus be what creates her tragic appeal, but even by Žižek's 1998 standards, one has to conclude that this makes her unsuitable as a model for transformative ethico-political action.

Unless, of course, one reinterprets her in a substantial way. But then a certain paradox emerges: Antigone can only function as a model for *radical* political action on the condition that she is stripped of her *radically* inhuman (anti-social and anti-political) desire. Žižek's selection of certain terms ("risk," "momentary suspension") seems to perform this function of socializing/politicizing Antigone's pure desire. The tension here is between an admiration for Antigone's pure desire and a simultaneous need to *give way* on her radical desire in order to make it relevant for politics. This is a tension that Žižek himself has accepted as far as his earlier work is concerned — consider, for example, *The Metastases of Enjoyment*, in which he acknowledges, in a self-critical tone, that in the past he has yielded to the "temptation" of complementing or moderating Lacan's ethics of persisting in one's desire.[17] Judging from his 1998 *Umbr(a)* article, we can conclude that the tension may be displaced and camouflaged, but not fully resolved.

If Antigone is useful only if reinterpreted in such a way — a way almost antithetical to her profile in the play — why should we retain her as a paradigm of the ethico-political act? *Wouldn't the truly ethical act be to traverse the lure of Antigone altogether?*

This is not to say that the problem lies entirely with Žižek's appropriation of Lacan's commentary and the figure of Antigone. The problem is also the exclusive attention given to the *Ethics* seminar. *Clearly, Antigone is not Lacan's last — or most insightful — word on the question of ethics.* His position continued to develop in a direction that undermined his earlier focus on Antigone's pure desire. As Alenka Zupančič has pointed out, this becomes evident, for example, in *The Four Fundamental Concepts of Psychoanalysis*, where the idea of "pure desire" is radically questioned.[18] Indeed, here Lacan not only denies the possibility of a pure desire of the analyst, but also highlights the alienating character of desire — *"man's desire is the desire of the Other"*[19] — while also pointing to the interpenetration of law and desire.[20] This shift needs to be taken into account when discussing the function of Antigone. Let us examine in more detail some of its implications.

Lacan's reading of Antigone in the *Ethics* seminar is based on the antithesis between Creon's ethics of "the good of all,"[21] and Antigone's ethics, which is articulated around "a good that is different from everyone else's,"[22] a pure (and thus deadly) incarnation of the "laws of desire." But is this opposition as radical as it seems at first? What is the exact nature of the antithesis between Creon and Antigone in Lacan's account? It is primarily an opposition between the order (and the morality) of power and an ethics of pure desire. Creon's morality is the traditional morality also supported by Aristotle: it "is the morality of the master, created for the virtues of the master and linked to the order of powers."[23] This order is not to become the object of contempt; Lacan makes clear that his comments are not those of an anarchist, but simply of someone aware of the *limits* of this order. In the *Ethics* seminar, these limits are understood in terms of desire: what is opposed to traditional ethics is the pole of desire.[24] The position of power *vis-à-vis* desire has always been the same: "'Let it be clear to everyone that this is on no account the moment to express the least surge of desire.' The morality of power, of the service of goods, is as follows: 'As far as desires are concerned, come back later. Make them wait.'"[25]

In this schema, Antigone's pure desire becomes the model of a radical transgression of the suppression or gentrification of desire implicit in every power structure and in the moral order sustaining it. Desire is posited as the complete antithesis of the sphere of the goods, as the transgression of power in all its different forms (capitalist or communist):

> Part of the world has resolutely turned in the direction of the service of goods, thereby rejecting everything that has to do with the relationship of man to desire — it is what is known as the postrevolutionary perspective. The only thing to be said is that people don't seem to have realized that, by formulating things in this way, one is simply perpetuating the eternal tradition of power, namely, "Let's keep on working, and as far as desire is concerned, come back later." But what does it matter? In this tradition the communist future is only different from Creon's, from that of the city, in assuming — and it's not negligible — that the sphere of goods to which we must all devote ourselves may at some point embrace the whole universe.[26]

While Lacan's insightful critique of the communist utopia remains important, it is clear that his positing of desire as the antithesis of the order of power and of the service of goods cannot be sustained. It probably belongs to what Žižek has correctly criticized as a "false transgression," which ultimately reproduces the order that it is supposed to undermine. In fact, it is Lacan himself who provides the theoretical tools for such a critique of his earlier work, particularly of his comments on Antigone. It is Lacan who highlights the constitutive dialectic between law and desire. In his unpublished seminar on anxiety, delivered only two years after the *Ethics* seminar, one finds a revealing passage: "desire and the law, which appear to be opposed in a relationship of antithesis, are only one and the same barrier to bar our access to the thing. *Nolens, volens*: desiring, I commit myself to the path of the law."[27] Desire not only loses its value as a pure force of transgression, but is also revealed as the ultimate support of power and the order of goods. As soon as jouissance acquires its central place in Lacan's theoretical universe, desire is revealed as a defense against enjoyment, as a compromise formation, while drive emerges as the nodal point of his ethical thought.[28] In that sense, desire can never be a pure transgressive force. Even in perversion, where desire "appears by presenting itself as what lays down the law, namely as a subversion of the law, it is in fact well and truly the support of a law."[29] *Desire is the law.*[30] It is thus not surprising that Antigone eventually links her desire to a certain law, the laws of the gods: "These laws — I was not about to break them, not out of fear of some man's [Creon's] wounded pride, and face the retribution of the gods."[31]

Hence it is not only the order of power that is limited; desire also has precise *limits*.[32] It is always conditioned by the structures of fantasy sustaining "hegemonic" regimes — regimes of power, consumption, and even resistance and transgression. It is always stimulated by the imaginary lure of attaining jouissance, but it is also sustained by the constitutive inability to realize such a goal. In that sense, desire "succeeds," reproduces itself, through its own failure. This reproduction is not politically innocent. Consumer culture, for example, is partly sustained by the continuous displacement of final satisfaction from advertisement to advertisement, from product to product, from fantasy to fantasy. The important "by-product" of this play is a specific structuration of desire which guarantees, through its cumulative metonymic effect, the reproduction of the market economy within a distinct "promotional culture."[33]

It is Lacan himself who points the way to traversing the lure of Antigone by shifting his understanding of desire. This shift needs to be acknowledged as the radical break it truly represents. Any attempt to reconcile the "pure" desire of Antigone with the later conceptualization and the critique of illusory desire and/or the ethics of desire with the ethics of the drive — what Zupančič seems to attempt in the last pages of her *Ethics of the Real* — needs to be re-examined and further debated.[34]

III.

Let us return to Žižek's discussion of Antigone. His paradoxical idealization of Antigone as a model of radical ethico-political action seems also to conflict with his own Lacanian account of the act as a non-subjective, non-intentional encounter with the real. Antigone's act is clearly an act of "subjective" autonomy beyond the restrictions of the social world. Isn't it the case, then, that Antigone's "heroic" act conflicts with Žižek's conceptualization of the act as distinct from Will?[35] In the *Umbr(a)* text, he makes abundantly clear that the "act as object is also to be opposed to the subject...This act is precisely something which unexpectedly 'just occurs.' It is an occurrence which most surprises its agent itself."[36] In *L'acte psychoanalytique*, Lacan himself points out that the act entails a certain "renewal" of the subject[37] — the act is never an act of which anyone can claim to be the master.[38] Is this really compatible with Antigone's stance? If Žižek's position is that "absolute/unconditional acts do occur, but not in the idealist guise of a self-transparent gesture performed by a subject with a pure will who fully intends them,"[39] then Antigone seems to have no place in his schema. What is needed instead is a non-subjective formal model of the act. What would such a model look like? When Žižek juxtaposes deconstruction with psychoanalysis, it seems that he is indirectly attempting a reply. How does Žižek conceptualize the distinction between the deconstructionist and Lacanian positions? In order to ground his ethics of the political, it seems that he introduces a criterion in terms of the oppositions passivity/activity and negativity/positivity and their philosophical/religious mutations: finitude/immortality and lack/miracle. In short, Žižek's point is that deconstruction prioritizes lack and finitude as the limit of ethico-political action, and locates the source of evil in any attempt to surpass the subject's constitutive division and act like God. In stark opposition to such a pessimistic standpoint, Žižek's response is to reverse the argument, making the true source of evil the assumption of finitude, mortality, and lack as such, ignoring the dimension of "divine miracles." Let us examine in more detail the terms of this opposition.

First, it is not entirely clear why anyone would associate the logic of lack — of constitutive lack as the support and limit of desire, as its condition of possibility and impossibility — with deconstruction. Lack and its various synonyms, lack in its various guises, is clearly a Lacanian concept, as Žižek himself has pointed out repeatedly. In *The Sublime Object of Ideology*, for example, one finds the following quotation with respect to the importance of lack, specifically the "lack in the Other": "Today, it is a commonplace that the Lacanian subject is divided, crossed-out, identical to a lack in the signifying chain. However, the most radical dimension of Lacanian theory lies not in recognizing this fact but in realizing that the big Other, the symbolic order itself, is also *barré*, crossed-out, by a fundamental impossibility, structured around an impossible/traumatic kernel."[40] In his *Umbr(a)* text, however, lack and division paradoxically reappear as internal moments of the deconstructionist ethics of finitude. In Žižek's recent book on totalitarianism, what sounds like the lack in the Other is treated in a similar way: "The deconstructionist political doxa goes something like this: the social is the field of structural undecidability, it is marked by an irreducible gap or lack, forever condemned to non-identity with itself; and 'totalitarianism' is, at its most elementary, the closure of this undecidability."[41] It is difficult to understand why Žižek attributes to deconstruction what he himself has described as "the most radical dimension of Lacanian theory," the lack in the socio-symbolic Other, as well as the Lacanian "commonplace" of the subject as lack. One can only speculate that this move, visible in many of Žižek's recent texts, must be related to a general *political* strategy of juxtaposing negativity and positivity, passivity and activity, pessimism and optimism. If his version of radical politics is to be presented as an optimistic politics of the miraculous act — a politics of almost vitalist activity — and if Lacanian theory is to be presented as a support of this politics, then it has to be purified of its stress on negativity and lack.

The problem, however, is that even this purification fails to guarantee the theoretico-political coherence of Žižek's argument. Passivity, for example, survives to haunt his politics of the act. Even if lack were to be associated with deconstruction, does that transform the supposedly "Lacanian" politics of the miraculous act to a politics beyond passivity? I doubt it, precisely because, as we have seen, the act is not subjective or subjectivized. According to Žižek's own schema, our relation to acts is always a relation of assumption, of coming to terms with them: "*there are acts...they do occur* and...we have to come to terms with them."[42] What, then, is the difference between assuming lack and assuming the act, the event? The only difference seems to be located in the particular content of each experience — and thus Žižek's argument passes from a more formal level to a level conditioned by concrete experience and its contingent symbolization/evaluation. Let's see how. Žižek's argument relies on the opposition between lack, denoting finitude and negativity, and divine miracle, denoting immortality and positivity. The position Žižek wants to attack is the one that advocates an assumption of lack and negativity, while the position he wants to defend conceptualizes the act as a miraculous event: "[acts] occur, on the contrary, as a totally unpredictable *tuche*, a miraculous event which shatters our lives. To put it in somewhat pathetic terms, this is how the 'divine' dimension is present in our lives."[43] Is it possible, however, to sustain such a sharp distinction? I see at least two problems with such a position: one theoretical, the other political. At the theoretical level, it is impossible to ignore the irreducible interconnection between negativity and positivity, lack and desire, death and resurrection. Even in Alain Badiou's work, which seems to be the source of Žižek's conception of the event here, the event refers to a real break that destabilizes a given discursive articulation, a pre-existing order.[44] It has, in other words, a negative/disruptive dimension. It creates a lack in the pre-existing structure. But like Ernesto Laclau's *dislocation*, it also entails a positive dimension. In Badiou the dislocating event is what (potentially) produces a new form of subjectivity. In that sense, the dimension of the "miracle" — if one wants to use such religious jargon — is most visible in the continuous "transubstantiation" of negative into positive. This interconnection is constitutive of social and political life, and this is not only an ethical but primarily an analytical/empirical observation.

Furthermore, by simplifying the terms of a complex relation, Žižek — at least in his argument — links theory to political experience in a reductive way. The destabilization of the absolute frontiers between positive and negative is bound to contaminate the idea of miracle itself. The implication is that any prioritization of the field of miracles has to confront the question of how to distinguish between true and false, divine and satanic miracles.[45] We already know this from Christian theology, Church history, and everyday life in religious communities. We also know it from the critique of Badiou's work. In Jean-Jacques Lecercle's words: "I can find hardly anything within [Badiou's] system to protect me from Heidegger's mistake, when he took the National Socialist 'revolution' for an event, and thought that a new process of truth had started. The risk is that the eventuality of the event will eventually be left to subjective decision."[46] Simon Critchley similarly asks: "how and in virtue of what is one to distinguish a true event from a false event? That is, I don't see how — on the basis of Badiou's criteria — we could ever distinguish a true event from a false event."[47] Badiou's "event" and Žižek's "act" seem to suffer from the same limitation: as soon as we accept a strict differentiation between positive and negative, good and bad, as soon as we prioritize one of these poles by disavowing the continuous interpenetration between positivity and negativity, we merely displace the problem into the realm of concrete ethico-political experience. *However, the larger problem is that we lose at the same time every theoretical/symbolic resource capable of supporting a proper ethical attitude in this unavoidable encounter with the real.*

As we have seen, Žižek's conceptualization of a politics of the act seems to be premised on the idea that the assumption of lack and finitude within a political project of social transformation can have only disastrous or crippling results. Indeed, postmodern pessimism is a problem, but is it to be resolved through a reoccupation of quasi-religious faith? Is it to be resolved through the utopian disavowal of lack and negativity in political discourse? This option is clearly open to us, but it is difficult to see how it would be different from the "false transgression" stigmatized by Žižek. It is also obvious that it would expose the politics of social transformation into an unacceptable risk of *absolutization*. Thus, in opposition to Žižek's strict differentiation between the ethics of assuming lack and a politics of the act, why not see the assumption/institutionalization of the lack in the Other not as a limit but as the condition of possibility, or in any case a crucial resource, in ethically assuming the radical character of an act, of relating ourselves — as divided beings — to an event. Isn't something like that happening, for example, when we fall in love, one of the privileged fields in which events take place in Badiou's view? Although a degree of chance is always operative, falling in love is never merely a chance event. It presupposes a certain preparedness. As Darian Leader reminds us, it has precise conditions of possibility linked to a sense of discontent, incompleteness, and lack.[48] Similarly, though the cases are not entirely symmetrical, even if "the act as real is an event which occurs *ex nihilo*, without any fantasmatic support,"[49] *assuming* this act nevertheless entails traversing the fantasy and the assumption of the lack. This is the symbolic matrix within which ethically assuming the act can become possible.[50] This is perhaps what we can learn from the psychoanalytic act as an act that presupposes a certain reflexivity, an awareness of its own limits, of the fact that it will never lead to the full realization of subjectivity (neither of the analyst nor of the analysand)[51]: in the beginning of every new analysis, the analyst authorizes and *risks* an operation, through the institution of the subject supposed to know, knowing well that it will end with his or her own rejection as excrement.[52] Only thus can the analyst's assumption of castration and division be *re-enacted* in the subjective structure of the analysand.

As Žižek himself has pointed out in another text, "[t]here is ethics — that is to say, an injunction which cannot be grounded in ontology — in so far as there is a crack in the ontological edifice of the universe: at its most elementary, ethics designates fidelity to this crack."[53] In order for a truly ethical fidelity to an event to become possible, another fidelity is presupposed — a fidelity that cannot be reduced to the event itself or to particular symbolizations of the event, a fidelity to *event-ness* as distinct from particular events, a "fidelity to the Real *qua* impossible."[54] Such a standpoint not only presents the necessary symbolic preparations for the proper ethical reception of the act/event, but also offers our best defense against the ever-present risk of being lured by a false event, a satanic miracle, against the ever-present risk of terror and *absolutization* of an event, to use Badiou's vocabulary.[55] Of course, one should be aware that fidelity to eventness, to what ultimately permits the emergence of the new and makes possible the assumption of an act, presupposes a certain betrayal, not of the act itself, but of a certain rendering of the act as an absolute and divine positivity. In that sense, fidelity to an event can flourish and avoid absolutization only as an *infidel fidelity*, only within the framework of another fidelity — fidelity to the openness of the political space and to the awareness of the constitutive impossibility of a final suture of the social — within the framework of a commitment to the continuous political re-inscription of the irreducible lack in the Other.[56]

Needless to say, I am not offering these reflections as some kind of final statement regarding the issues discussed here. The transformative potential of a Lacanian ethics of the political is a crucial issue that is far from settled. Furthermore, bringing event-ness into consideration renders possible the restructuring of the formal requirements of an ethico-political conception of the act in what some would call a radical democratic direction without yet being able to bridge the gap between theory and politics.[57] This irreducible aporia is, I think, what ultimately explains Žižek's choice to persist in his references to Antigone as an embodiment of a particular ethico-political position within a formal framework essentially alien or even antithetical to her. But the ethical fidelity to acts/events, which is the point of *Antigone* is clearly not embodied by its title character. *It is rather embodied by tragedy itself as a genre, as a social institution staging again and again the suspension of the socio-symbolic order and permitting a thorough self-reflection on the political order of the city and its moral foundations.*[58] It is not Antigone but Sophocles who fulfills the criteria set out at the beginning of Žižek's 1998 text. It is the tragedian who assumes and re-inscribes radical socio-political critique within the heart of the city, reproducing democratic society by re-examining again and again — through a series of aesthetico-political *re-acts* — its ethico-political premises. As Jean-Pierre Vernant explains: "What tragedy is talking about is itself [the city, Athens] and the problems of law it is encountering. What is talking and what is talked about is the audience on the benches, but first of all it is the City...which puts itself on the stage and plays itself...Not only does the tragedy enact itself on stage...it enacts its own problematics. It puts in question its own internal contradictions, revealing...that the true subject matter of tragedy is social thought...in the very process of elaboration."[59]

I would like to thank Vassilis Lambropoulos, Jason Glynos, and the *Umbr(a)* editorial collective for their valuable comments on an earlier draft of this essay.

1. Jacques Lacan, *The Seminar of Jacques Lacan, Book VII: The Ethics of Psychoanalysis, 1959-1960*, ed. Jacques-Alain Miller, trans. Dennis Porter (New York: Norton, 1992), 3.

2. Slavoj Žižek, "From 'Passionate Attachments' to Dis-Identification," *Umbr(a)* 1 (1998): 3-17. Parts of this text are included in "Passionate (Dis)Attachments, or, Judith Butler as a Reader of Freud," in *The Ticklish Subject: The Absent Centre of Political Ontology* (London: Verso, 1999), 247-312.

3. Žižek, "From 'Passionate Attachments' to Dis-Identification," 5.

4. Lacan, *L'acte psychanalytique* (1967-1968), unpublished seminar, trans. Cormac Gallagher. In this seminar, the paradoxical status of the act as *un fait de significant*, as a language and division effect, is illuminated in depth. Furthermore, the relation between psychoanalysis and politics occupies a prominent place. Not only does Lacan discuss the status of the political act with reference to Lenin, among others, and the "days of October," but the final sessions of the seminar are also disrupted by the events of May 1968. Respecting the strike called by the SNES (the Union of Teachers in Higher Education), Lacan would in fact suspend his teaching for two sessions of the seminar (8 and 15 May 1968) and offer instead a brief but extremely interesting commentary on the way analysts could become "worthy of the events." But this is also the seminar in which the analyst's "refusal to act," which frustrates the demand of the analysand, is given appropriate attention.

5. Lacan, *The Ethics of Psychoanalysis*, 282.

6. Žižek, "From 'Passionate Attachments' to Dis-Identification," 6.

7. Ibid., 6-7. The example of Antigone is of considerable importance in Žižek's recent work. See, for example, *Did Somebody Say Totalitarianism? Five Interventions in the (Mis)use of a Notion* (London: Verso, 2001), esp. ch. 4.

8. Žižek, "From 'Passionate Attachments' to Dis-Identification," 7.

9. Ibid., 9.

10. Ibid., 16.

11. Ibid., 17.

12. Simon Critchley, *Ethics—Politics—Subjectivity: Essays on Derrida, Levinas and Contemporary French Thought* (London: Verso, 1999), 231.

13. Sophocles, *Antigone*, in *The Three Theban Plays*, trans. Robert Fagles (New York: Penguin, 1984), 102.

14. Lacan, *The Ethics of Psychoanalysis*, 281.

15. Ibid., 271.

16. Žižek, *The Metastases of Enjoyment: Six Essays on Woman and Causality* (London: Verso, 1994), 69.

17. Ibid., 84.

18. Alenka Zupančič, *Ethics of the Real: Kant, Lacan* (London: Verso, 2000), 3.

19. Lacan, *The Seminar of Jacques Lacan, Book XI: The Four Fundamental Concepts of Psychoanalysis*, ed. Jacques-Alain Miller, trans. Alan Sheridan (New York: Norton, 1981), 38.

20. Ibid., 34.

21. Lacan, *The Ethics of Psychoanalysis*, 258.

22. Ibid., 270.

23. Ibid., 315.

24. Ibid., 314.

25. Ibid., 315.

26. Ibid., 318.

27. Lacan, *L'angoisse* (1962-1963), unpublished seminar, trans. Cormac Gallagher, 19 December 1962.

28. See Zupančič, 235.

29. Lacan, *L'angoisse*, 27 February 1963.

30. Ibid.

31. Sophocles, 82.

32. Lacan, *The Four Fundamental Concepts of Psychoanalysis*, 31.

33. For an analysis of advertising discourse along these lines, see Yannis Stavrakakis, "On the Critique of Advertising Discourse: A Lacanian View," *Third Text* 51 (2000), 85-90.

34. Undoubtedly desire and drive are related, but their relation seems to me to escape any logic of *reconciliation* or *supplementation*, which is how Zupančič ultimately views their relation. Her aim seems to be to "reconcile" desire with drive, something attempted through presenting drive as a "supplement" of desire: "at the heart of desire a possible passage opens up towards the drive; one might therefore come to the drive if one follows the 'logic' of desire to its limit" (Zupančič, 238, 239, 243). What is not given appropriate attention here is that reaching this limit entails a *crossing* which radically transforms our relation to desire. In other words, the limit of desire does not connote the *automatic* passage into a supplementary field of reconciliation; it primarily signifies a rupture, precisely because, as Jacques-Alain Miller points out, "desire never goes beyond a certain point." Whereas Lacan's early work and his conceptualization of desire as something "always in violation, always rebellious and diabolical" — a position informing his reading of Antigone — leads to "the confusion between the drive and desire," as soon as desire is reconceptualized as ultimately submissive to a law, a shift of almost "gigantic" proportions is instituted, and this shift must be acknowledged thoroughly. See Miller, "Commentary on Lacan's Text" in *Reading Seminars I and II: Lacan's Return to Freud*, ed. Richard Feldstein, Bruce Fink, and Maire Jaanus (Albany: State University of New York Press, 1996), 422-423.

35. See Žižek, *The Plague of Fantasies* (London: Verso, 1997), 223.

36. Žižek, "From 'Passionate Attachments' to Dis-Identification," 14.

37. Lacan, *L'acte psychanalytique*, 29 November 1967.

38. Ibid., 24 January 1968.

39. Žižek, "From 'Passionate Attachments' to Dis-Identification," 16-17.

40. Žižek, *The Sublime Object of Ideology* (London: Verso, 1989), 122.

41. Žižek, *Did Somebody Say Totalitarianism?*, 6.

42. Žižek, "From 'Passionate Attachments' to Dis-Identification," 15.

43. Ibid., 17.

44. Many of Žižek's theoretical choices and devices in this and other recent texts seem to be conditioned by a reading of Alain Badiou. The language of *immortality* and *miracles*, for example, is much closer to Badiou than to Lacan. It is true that some of Badiou's work comes very close to a Lacanian problematic and introduces a refreshing tone in contemporary philosophy, which explains the references to his work by Lacanian theorists such as Žižek, Zupančič, and Joan Copjec. However, there are many areas where Badiou follows a direction that seems incompatible with Lacanian political theory. I attempt to highlight some of these

incompatibilities in "Re-activating the Democratic Revolution: The Politics of Transformation Beyond Reoccupation and Conformism," *Parallax*, in press.

45. In *L'acte psychanalytique*, Lacan indirectly raises this issue when he discusses the relation between the symptomatic and the psychoanalytic act (see the lecture of 22 November 1967).

46. Jean-Jacques Lecercle, "Cantor, Lacan, Mao, *même combat*: The Philosophy of Alain Badiou," *Radical Philosophy* 93 (1999): 12.

47. Critchley, "Demanding Approval: On the Ethics of Alain Badiou," *Radical Philosophy* 100 (2000): 23.

48. See Darian Leader, *Promises Lovers Make When it Gets Late* (London: Faber & Faber, 1997).

49. Žižck, "From 'Passionate Attachments' to Dis-Identification," 14.

50. Ironically, even Antigone's act is partly conditioned by an acceptance of finitude. In her own words, "Die I must, I've known it all my life — how could I keep from knowing? — even without your death-sentence ringing in my ears. And if I am to die before my time I consider that a gain" (Sophocles, 82).

51. Lacan, *L'acte psychanalytique*, 20 March 1968.

52. Ibid., 21 February 1968.

53. Žižek, *The Plague of Fantasies*, 214.

54. Ibid., 215.

55. See Badiou, *Ethics: An Essay on the Understanding of Evil*, trans. Peter Hallward (London: Verso, 2001), 85.

56. This is how I translate in political terms Lacan's discussion of the psychoanalytic act as an assertion that institutes a space permitting continuous "re-acts." See Lacan, *L'acte psychanalytique*, 20 March 1968.

57. As Lacan puts it, "the theoretician is not the one who finds the way. He explains it. Obviously, the explanation is useful to find the rest of the path" (Ibid., 19 June 1968).

58. As far as Sophocles' *Antigone* is concerned, such a logic seems to be embodied by the two figures, Haemon and Tiresias, who are strangely foreclosed in most discussions of the tragedy in order to sustain the seductive lure of the Creon-Antigone couple.

59. Jean-Pierre Vernant, "Greek Tragedy: Problems of Interpretation," in *The Structuralist Controversy*, ed. Richard Macksey and Eugenio Donato (Baltimore: Johns Hopkins University Press, 1972), 278-279.

"WHAT SOME WOULD CALL...":
A RESPONSE TO YANNIS STAVRAKAKIS
slavoj žižek

My first reaction to Yannis Stavrakakis' critical essay is one of perplexion: how can it contain so many false attributions? If I were to answer it properly, I would first have to engage in the tedious exercise of point-by-point demonstration, by way of extensive quotation, of how what he presents as my position is simply not mine. Stavrakakis writes, for example, *"Clearly, Antigone is not Lacan's last — or most insightful — word on the question of ethics.* His position continued to develop [after the *Ethics* seminar] in a direction that undermined his earlier focus on Antigone's pure desire." Agreed, but why is this written as an argument against me? Did I not develop *in extenso* Lacan's shift from pure desire to drive? Did I not elaborate in detail a shift of "primary examples" from Antigone to Sygne de Coufontaine (from Claudel's *L'otage*) and Medea? And how can the assertion of the identity of law and desire (*"Desire is the law,"* he emphasizes) be an argument against me when I have made this point so often that I myself am already tired of it? Stavrakakis asserts that I am guilty of "juxtaposing negativity and positivity, passivity and activity, pessimism and optimism," and that I thereby neglect the "irreducible interconnection between negativity and positivity, lack and desire, death and resurrection," that is, the fact that the act has "a negative/disruptive dimension," that it involves a "continuous 'transubstantiation' of negative into positive" — is this meant seriously? Is not the *title* of one of my books *Tarrying With the Negative*, that is, the notion that negativity should gain positive existence? Do I not reproach Badiou for neglecting the link between death and resurrection in his reading of Christianity, as well as for missing the point of the philosophical assertion of finitude as a transcendental category? Do I not emphasize how the act is, in its innermost negative, a "No," a disruption of the existing socio-symbolic order? (With regard to Badiou, however, I should emphasize that I do not subscribe to the rather mundane reproach that he cannot provide clear criteria for distinguishing false from true events, and thus avoid, say, Heidegger's mistaking Nazism for a true event. Badiou's insistence that an event — in contrast to a pseudo-event — intervenes within a situation from the point of its "symptomal torsion" has at least to be given a fair hearing.) So again, *why* such an egregious misreading? Is it not that Stavrakakis' own argument is twisted by what — to quote him — "some would call a radical democratic direction"?

What is truly at stake in his attack? Two interconnected things, as far as I can see: the notion of the *political act* and the status of *democracy*. With regard to the act, Stavrakakis' starting point is my preference for the "tragic-heroic paradigm" as embodied by Antigone. But he fails to acknowledge that I also developed years ago the "comic" aspect of the Lacanian real, the fact that Christianity does *not* involve a tragic paradigm, as well as the key political fact that the "extreme" experiences of the twentieth century, holocaust and gulag, can no longer be defined as "tragic." If anything, it is Stavrakakis who opens up the space for a tragic paradigm. Is not what he calls the "absolutization" of the event, which leads to a *désastre*, the model of political tragedy? The catch, however, lies elsewhere. When Stavrakakis writes that "fidelity to an event can flourish and avoid absolutization only as an *infidel fidelity*, only within the framework of another fidelity — fidelity to the openness of the political space and to the awareness of the constitutive impossibility of a final suture of the social," he surreptitiously introduces a difference between the unconditional-ethical and the pragmatico-political: the original fact is the lack, which pertains to human finitude, and all positive acts always fall short of this primordial lack. Thus we have what Derrida calls the "unconditional ethical injunction," impossible to fulfill, and positive acts or interventions, which remain strategic.

My opposition to this stance is twofold:

1) The Lacanian "act" precisely *suspends* this gap. As Alenka Zupančič recently put it, acts are "impossible," not in the sense of "impossible *to* happen," but in the sense of an "impossible *that* happened." *This* is why Antigone was of interest to me: her act is not a strategic intervention that maintains the gap separating her from the impossible Void — it rather "absolutely" enacts the Impossible. I am well aware of the "lure" of such an act, but I claim that, in Lacan's later versions of the act, this moment of "madness" beyond strategic intervention remains. In this precise sense, not only does the notion of the act not contradict the "lack in the Other," which, according to Stavrakakis, I neglect, it directly presupposes it. It is only through an act that I effectively assume the big Other's inexistence, that is, I enact the impossible, namely what appears as impossible within the coordinates of the existing socio-symbolic order.

2) There *are* (also) political acts — that is, politics cannot be reduced to the level of strategic-pragmatic interventions. In a radical political act, the opposition between a "crazy," destructive gesture and a strategic political decision momentarily breaks down, which is

why it is theoretically and politically wrong to oppose strategic political acts, as risky as they can be, to radical "suicidal" gestures *à la* Antigone, gestures of pure self-destructive ethical insistence with no apparent political goal. The point is not simply that, once we are thoroughly engaged in a political project, we are ready to put everything at stake for it, inclusive of our lives, but more precisely, that *only such an "impossible" gesture of pure expenditure can change the very coordinates of what is strategically possible within a historical constellation.* This is the key point: an act is neither a strategic intervention *into* the existing order, nor is it its "crazy," destructive *negation*; an act is an "excessive," trans-strategic intervention which redefines the rules and contours of the existing order.

So what about the reproach that Antigone does not only risk death or suspend the symbolic order — my determination of a political act — but that she actively strives for death, symbolic and real death, thereby displaying a purity of desire beyond any socio-political transformative action? First, is Antigone's act really outside of politics, and therefore "apolitical"? Is not her defiance to the order of the supreme power (Creon, who acts on behalf of the common good) political, albeit in a negative way? Is not, in certain extreme circumstances, such "apolitical" defiance on behalf of "decency" or "old customs" the very model of heroic political resistance? Second, Antigone's gesture is not simply a pure desire for death. If it were, she could have killed herself directly and spared the people around her all the fuss. Hers was not a pure symbolic striving for death, but an unconditional insistence on a particular symbolic ritual.

More generally, I have written extensively about how, far from being *the* seminar of Lacan, *The Ethics of Psychoanalysis* is rather the point of deadlock at which Lacan comes dangerously close to the standard version of the "passion of the Real." Do the unexpected echoes between this seminar and the thought of Georges Bataille, *the* philosopher of the passion of the Real if there ever was one, not unambiguously point in this direction? Is Lacan's ethical maxim "do not compromise your desire" (which, one should always bear in mind, would never appear again in his later work) not a version of Bataille's injunction "to think everything to a point that makes people tremble," to go as far as possible — to the point at which opposites coincide, at which infinite pain turns into the joy of highest bliss, at which the intensity of erotic enjoyment encounters death, at which sainthood overlaps with extreme dissolution, at which God himself is revealed as a cruel beast? Is the temporal coincidence of Lacan's seminar on ethics and Bataille's *Eroticism* more than mere coincidence? Is Bataille's domain of the Sacred, of the "accursed part," not his version of what, apropos *Antigone*, Lacan deployed as the domain of *Atè*? Does Bataille's opposition of "homogeneity," the order of exchange, and "heterogeneity," the order of limitless expenditure, not point towards Lacan's opposition of the order of symbolic exchange and the excess of the traumatic encounter with the real? And how can Bataille's elevation of the dissolute woman to the status of God not remind us of Lacan's claim that Woman is one of the names of God? This is not even to mention Bataille's term for the experience of transgression — impossible — which is Lacan's qualification of the real.

With regard to democracy, the first thing to admit is that, whatever one might accuse Lacan of, one cannot say he was a Leftist "democrat" in any meaningful sense of the term. As far as we can reconstruct his explicit political stance, he was a Gaullist; the basic thrust of his political remarks and reactions was always one of distrust of every democratic-emancipatory explosion. His message to the students of 1968 was that they were hysterics asking for a new Master, and that they would get one. *Seminar XVII* (on the four discourses) basically dismissed the student revolt as an index of the shift — internal to the capitalist order — toward the predominance of the university discourse. Whatever one wants to do with Lacan's theory, there is no way that one can claim that "radical democracy" is its direct implication.

At a more fundamental level, I think it is crucial to take note of the fact that, in the last decade and a half of his teaching, beginning with *Seminar XI*, Lacan struggled to overcome the Kantian horizon, the clearest indication of which is his reactualization of the concept of the drive. Drive functions beyond symbolic castration as an inherent detour or topological twist of the real itself. This shift in the late Lacan from a "transcendental" logic (symbolic castration as the ultimate horizon of our experience, emptying the place of the Thing and thus opening up the space for our desire) to a dimension "beyond castration" (a position which claims that beyond castration there is not simply the abyss of the Night of the Thing that swallows us) also has direct political consequences: if the "transcendental" Lacan can somehow be made into a "Lacan of democracy" (the empty place of Power for whose temporary occupancy multiple political subjects compete, against the "totalitarian" subject who claims to act directly for the Other's jouissance), the Lacan "beyond castration" points towards a post-democratic politics.

The problem I see is that all too many "radical" Leftists accept the legalistic logic of the "transcendental guarantee": they refer to democracy as the ultimate guarantee of those who are aware that there is no guarantee. That is to say, since no political act can claim a direct foundation in some transcendent figure of the big Other (of the "we are just instruments of a higher Necessity or Will" variety), since every such act involves the risk of a contingent decision, nobody has the right to impose his choice onto the others, which means that every collective choice has to be democratically legitimized. From this perspective, democracy is not so much the guarantee of the right choice as a kind of opportunistic insurance against possible failure: if things turn out wrong, I can always say we are all responsible. Consequently, I think that this last refuge has to be dropped and that one should fully assume the risk. The only adequate position is the "anti-essentialist" one advocated already by Lukács in his *History and Class Consciousness*: democratic struggle should not be fetishized; it is one form of struggle, and its choice should be determined by a global strategic assessment of circumstances, not by its immanent superior value.

Here one should be as clear as possible: with the rise of the anti-globalization movement, the era of the multitude of particular struggles that one should strive to link in a "chain of equivalences" is over. This struggle (the only serious opposition movement today) — whatever one's critical apprehensions towards it — is clearly focused on capitalism as a global system, and perceives all other struggles (for democracy, ecology, feminism, anti-racism, and so on) as subordinate.

CATCH ME IF YOU CAN
Dir. Steven Spielberg, 2002

I. "Catch Me If You Can": A Past Haunted by the Future

Steven Spielberg's most recent film, *Catch Me If You Can*, is an interesting departure from his earlier science fiction endeavors, *A.I.: Artificial Intelligence* and *Minority Report*. After two films set firmly in the future, *Catch Me If You Can* turns not merely to some vague historical past, but to an extremely particular, iconic historical moment: the mid-sixties in America, just prior to the cultural revolution of the late sixties and the rising political tensions that accompanied the civil rights movement and active opposition to the Vietnam War. A surface examination of the three would suggest that the two science fiction films must be future-driven, preoccupied with the possibilities of *what will happen*, while *Catch Me If You Can* must remain rigidly fixed in its loyalty to the past, locked in the memory of *what has happened*. In fact, the opposite is true; only the science fiction worlds that Spielberg imagines in the two earlier films are tied irrevocably to a lost past. Recall that for Detective John Anderton (Tom Cruise) in *Minority Report*, this lost past is a missing child and an estranged wife; for the robot-child David (Haley Joel Osment) in *A.I.*, what's lost is the mother, who drives him away after he has been programmed to love her.

In both films, any movement forward in time (the detective process in *Minority Report* and the mythical quest in *A.I.*) is governed by the character's attempt to recuperate this originary and defining loss. Take David for example, the robot-prototype programmed to love. He is adopted by a couple (whose real son is cryogenically frozen, awaiting a cure for his illness) and is "imprinted" to love by his new mother, Monica, through the repetition of a series of random, unrelated signifiers at the end of which she inserts her own name. Once his love for Monica takes hold, it is unrelenting; he is quite literally hardwired with an unending love. Eventually, of course, the couple's real son is cured and returns, and, after some sibling rivalry and several ridiculous mishaps, Monica drives David into the forest and leaves him there. Thus begins David's quest, which takes him literally to the end of the world (and, unbelievably, into the next one...) in order to find the Blue Fairy who will make him a real boy worthy of his lost mother's love.

This tale deserves attention because it allows us to make an important distinction between David's journey and that of Leonardo DiCaprio's character in *Catch Me If You Can*. At first, the narrative trajectories of the two boys' journeys might seem similar, but it turns out that the logic behind Frank W. Abagnale Jr.'s three-year spree of impersonation, forgery, and multi-million dollar check fraud is exactly the opposite of what drives David's 2,000+-year adventure. David's quest is truly mythical, that is, driven by the search for the lost origin: the moment at which both David and the world come into being, when Monica recites the words that imprint David with his love for her. It would be easy to read Frank Abagnale's story in the same terms: as a young man, he spends three years on a mad quest around the world trying to reconstruct the family he loses when, at sixteen, his parents decide to get divorced.

But there is a crucial difference: while David was driven out, prohibited from the fulfillment of his mother's love, *Frank runs*. He runs away from his home and his family. Furthermore, he runs at a key moment, the moment at which he is first confronted with the force that underlies the law, the force of the decision. Frank's mother explains, "there are laws — everything in this country has to be legal — so what we need to do is make some decisions,"[1] after which his father encourages, "Frank, just write down a name and this will all be over," and finally the lawyer says, "There is no wrong answer" (41). At this, Frank bolts. The remainder of the film, save the final thirty minutes or so, is contained in that thirty-second on-screen run; that is, it can be reduced to the logic of the run...well, that and perhaps the title of the film itself, which suggests that there is someone or something chasing him. So the question is: why does Frank run? What horrifies him? The answer to this question can't be underestimated because it determines how we see the rest of the movie.

This is the key, however: the answer cannot be a psychological one. Frank runs because he is confronted with the law, or rather, with the force that supports the law. The fact that "there is no wrong answer" to the question that is posed to him ("Mother or father?") suggests that the answer, the decision, comes from another place, that it can't be found within the law itself. It is this momentary glimpse of something beyond the law that horrifies Frank, causing him to run. To call Frank's adventure a quest is thus completely off the mark insofar as this would suggest that he seeks something. If David chases after love, Frank is instead chased by not love, but the law. This little switch — from love to the law — changes everything; it certainly destroys any simple notion that we have about the past and the future and how they operate in the two films. Perhaps it should be formulated like this: if *A.I.* is a film set in a future haunted by the past, *Catch Me If You Can* is a film set in a past haunted by the future.

II. "Frank W. Abagnale, Jr."

Strangely for a Spielberg project, *Catch Me If You Can* is not a movie about character relations (deep emotional and psychological struggles, complex character interactions), but rather about relations merely at the level of symbolic identity. Steve Melton, the film's propmaster explains, "In one of my first meetings with Steven Spielberg, he was very, very clear that this all [the checks, badges, forms, licenses, and so on] has to be perfect because he was really going to use the documents to tell the story" (103). Not only do the documents tell the story, but the film is, fundamentally, a story about documents rather than characters — or more precisely, the documents and the characters have exactly the same status. For this movie, a man is only as good as...not his word, nor even his bank account, but rather the name printed on his checks:

> FRANK SR.: I opened a checking account in your name. I put twenty-five dollars in the account so you can buy whatever you want. Don't tell your mother.
> Frank slowly opens the CHECKBOOK, sees his name at the top of the first check. [Here, Frank comments, "They've even got my name on them, huh?"]
> FRANK: But they turned down your loan?
> FRANK SR.: Yeah. They all turned me down.
> FRANK: So why open a bank account with them?
> FRANK SR.: Because one day you'll want something from these people — a house, a car — they have all the money. There's fifty checks here, Frank, which means from this day on — you're in their little club. (30-31)

Thus marks Frank's entry into the symbolic (significantly, the event takes place on young Frank's sixteenth birthday, the symbolic mark of his entrance into the adult world). At this point, Frank Sr. is allowing for his son's entrance into the very "little club" from which he has been expelled. The father is broke, is being pursued by the IRS, has been turned down for a loan, and is in danger of losing his business; he has defaulted on his status in the system of symbolic exchange. The younger Frank's own entry into the symbolic thus comes by way of a father who can neither maintain his own place within the system, nor, certainly, muster the strength to incarnate the force of the law. As a result, Frank Jr. encounters a law already missing its other side, the force or threat that supports it. The symbolic is strictly cut off from the force of the real, so not only does the law lack its superegoic reverse side, but the signifier is also detached from any reference to the real thing. Thus, young Frank is not interpellated into the symbolic; rather, he is "minted" into it. The signifier "Frank W. Abagnale, Jr." enters circulation the same way money does, unhinged from its reference to any "real" value.

The truth of the film, then, comes down to the transmission of documents. Instead of the movement and development of characters, we get an entire film about the passing of checks. This should be taken quite literally: Frank becomes a pilot not to make his father proud, or to get girls, or to travel to exotic places (all those things that might motivate a *character*), but because *being a pilot makes it easy to cash checks*. What this means for the film is that any action, relationship, or moment that casts Frank exclusively as a character is doomed to failure. The first situation that comes to mind here is the relationship between Frank and Brenda. By many accounts, this is the "one true relationship" and rests at the heart of the film, but Brenda must nevertheless betray Frank at the airport, forcing Frank to leave her behind. What is unusual about the scenario, however, is that first, Brenda's loyalty to Frank and her own innocence are sacrificed in the bargain, and second, Frank's leaving is a complete break, unrecuperated in the form of loss.

There is another, even more stunning, excising of character that occurs later in the film, one that might not have been apparent were it not for the publication of the screenplay. In this case, it concerns Frank's relationship with his mother, Paula (the film's other woman), and the scene in which Frank escapes from the plane that was returning him from France after his capture and runs to his mother's house. If *Catch Me If You Can* operated according to the logic of *A.I.* — the logic of love and loss — then Frank's crime spree truly would have been a quest, and this would have been the scene of its culmination. But what we find is that the scene that would have cast one of Frank's relationships into the abyss of loss is cut out of the film. According to the screenplay, upon returning to his mother's house and seeing her with her new husband and child, Frank is supposed to insist upon seeing his mother and then rush inside the house, where she reveals to him the truth about her marriage to his father — an unwanted pregnancy, a forced marriage, a premature baby, and so on — ending with the police finally catching up with him again:

THE SIRENS ARE DEAFENING NOW — THE LIGHTS AND SOUNDS FROM THE POLICE CARS FILLING THE HOUSE — THE DRIVEWAY AND FRONT LAWN FLOODED WITH POLICE AND FBI CARS —
Paula slowly stands, leads Frank over to the couch and sits him down. She covers him with a blanket — then kisses him on the head —
PAULA: You go to sleep now, Frank. (146)

But there is some reason that *this* scene cannot exist in *this* film, and that it ultimately gets cut. As it turns out, Frank never meets with or talks to his mother again and never enters the house; but instead, he turns around and rushes to surrender himself to the police, that is, to Carl Hanratty (Tom Hanks), the film's second father. Now Spielberg certainly doesn't object to this kind of scene of perverse/sublime (re-)union of the mother and son since, in *A.I.*, a similar moment marks the end of David's quest. Nevertheless, in the later film, the love of the mother (like that of Brenda) has to be sacrificed in the name of the film. (It is interesting to note that the reverse is true of *A.I.*, where one can't help but notice that, in its closing gesture of resurrecting the lost object, *the film itself is sacrificed* in order to preserve the love of the mother.) In Frank's case, ecstatic union with the mother will not answer his question; in fact, given the nature of Frank's entry into the symbolic, the mother's love is virtually incomprehensible to him, like something that exists in another world.

What we *do* find in this scene as it actually plays out in *Catch Me If You Can* is a repeat of that earlier scene that set Frank running: the founding decision of "mother or father?" In this case, the father is not the first (already symbolically, and now really) dead father, but rather the second, surrogate father, the incarnation of the law itself. The decision here can't be reduced simply to a choice between love (the mother) or the law (the father). Frank is confronted with a choice between two horrors, which is to say, a choice between two registers of love: love in the real and love in the symbolic. The second father does what the first could not: he embodies the force of the law, and he finally catches up with Frank by cornering him up against a worse threat, the threat of the real. If the moment with the mother cannot put an end to Frank's running, we get another scene in its place, a confrontation with the paradoxical force of the law, with love in the symbolic.

What comes to mark the end of Frank's running is not a moment of absolute fullness but rather one of complete emptiness. The scene occurs after Hanratty has taken Frank out of prison and put him back to work within the law, namely in the FBI's check fraud division. Now free to keep running, Frank heads for the airport:

> Frank is wearing the PILOT'S UNIFORM as he walks through the endless tunnel that leads to the departure gates. A VOICE from behind stops him....
> HANRATTY: I'm gonna let you fly tonight. I won't even try and stop you because I know you'll be back on Monday.
> FRANK: Why would I come back?
> HANRATTY: Look around, Frank. Nobody is chasing you. (151-152)

And that's it: Frank doesn't run. The only one who can finally incarnate the force of the law is the one so powerful that he can relinquish all his power. "Catch me if you can" is a demand that could only come from one who doesn't know the true force of the law: that it holds you most tightly only when the chase stops.

—*Theresa Giron*

1.   Jeff Nathanson, *Catch Me If You Can*, ed. Linda Sunshine (New York: Newmarket, 2002), 40. Subsequent references to the screenplay will appear parenthetically within the text.

ANTIGONE'S CLAIM: KINSHIP BETWEEN LIFE AND DEATH
Judith Butler
(New York: Columbia University Press, 2000), 103 pp.

The eponymous heroine of Sophocles' *Antigone* has served for a number of writers and artists as a figure of resistance to seemingly insuperable oppression. Undoubtedly, the most famous twentieth-century examples are the stage adaptations by Jean Anouilh (1944) and Bertolt Brecht (1948). For their audiences, Antigone's refusal to heed Creon's edict that the remains of her traitorous brother be denied burial rites embodied a call for resistance to the Nazi occupation and the Vichy government. Some ten years later, Jacques Lacan returned to the play in his seventh seminar. There, too, the re-emergence of Antigone is arguably linked to a specific historical context: one might suggest that Lacan's choice to discuss Sophocles in *The Ethics of Psychoanalysis* was at least partially precipitated by the increasingly violent crisis that demanded the attention of French intellectuals and the French Left in the late 1950s. The *Ethics* seminar, after all, took place during 1959-1960, a time marked by the turmoil of Algerian resistance to French occupation and its consequent, brutal repression — a crisis that Frantz Fanon famously addresses in *A Dying Colonialism* (1959). Lacan's suggestion that *Antigone* anticipates "the cruelties of our time," offering "images of our modern wars," can clearly be read as a reference to the Algerian battle.[1]

Judith Butler's re-evaluation of *Antigone*'s legacy is similarly inspired by contemporary political concerns. The backdrop for *Antigone's Claim* is the increasingly conservative political climate in the United States, the book's most immediate target being the controversy surrounding non-heteronormative family arrangements and same-sex couples' right to adoption. Butler's stated aim in taking up *Antigone* is to revive radical politics that are not assimilable to, and that do not seek the legitimation of, existing formations of state power. For Butler, Antigone prefigures a politics that would "confront and defy the state" (1), while at the same time acknowledging the impossibility of claiming a voice "that might in any way be unimplicated in the very power that it opposes" (2). Butler argues that Antigone, in her stubborn disregard of Creon's orders, is not situated outside the *polis*, beyond the symbolic embodiment of the law. Instead, she is both inside and outside the city, "chiasmically related" (6, 8) to the law Creon represents. According to Butler, Antigone's resistance parasitically appropriates the language and idiom of the law that she defies. Her refusal functions "as an unanticipated appropriation and perversion of [the law's] own mandate" (54): "she absorbs the very language of the state against which she rebels, and hers becomes a politics not of oppositional purity but of the scandalously impure" (5). Consequently, "her autonomy is gained through the appropriation of the authoritative voice of the one she resists, and appropriation that has within it traces of a simultaneous refusal and assimilation of that very authority" (11).

In other words, Butler assigns to Antigone what she has famously identified as the insubordinate performativity enabled by the law's reiterative structure. Given the necessity for its incessant repetition, the law is open to being inaccurately repeated, performed in a way that diverts it from its intended orbit. Butler contrasts this reading to Lacan's, whose theory, she argues, poses insurmountable constraints to symbolic change. For her, Lacan's reading of Antigone blocks any possible interrogation of how one could reconfigure the symbolic realm. In Lacan's work, "the notion of the symbolic is limited by the description of its own transcendentalizing function." The symbolic "can acknowledge the contingency of its own structure only by disavowing the possibility of any substantial alteration in its field of operation" (30). According to Butler, Lacan reveals the symbolic as contingent only by shoring up its unassailability: the recognition of the law's non-essential nature works to constrain the subject more thoroughly in its circuits.

Butler insists that the law cannot operate without producing its own transgression. Discussing the influence of Lévi-Strauss' theory of kinship and the incest taboo on Lacan's notion of the symbolic, she asks: "can such a rule, understood as a prohibition, actually operate, however effectively, without producing and maintaining the specter of its transgression? Do such rules produce conformity, or do they also produce a set of social configurations that exceed and defy the rules by which they are occasioned?" (17). Butler's preferred rhetorical mode of erotesis[2] may obscure the fact that, for Lacan, the law never functions without generating its own transgression as excess jouissance. According to Lacan, tragedy is concerned precisely with this paradox. In the wake of the symbolic law, something else surfaces, something that is intimately tied to the logic of the law yet nevertheless radically opposed to it: "The good cannot reign over all without an excess emerging whose fatal consequences are revealed to us in tragedy" (*Ethics*, 259). This excess is the remainder of the real that is properly speaking not outside the law but internal to it, designating the point of its failure that is identical to its very possibility. While Creon is on the side of the symbolic, Antigone, in her obdurate insistence on giving her brother a proper burial, quickens this underside of the law, its internal limit. This internal outside, or "intimate exteriority" (*Ethics*, 139), allows the law's functioning yet insists in its circuits as an excessive, inassimilable ghost that continuously prevents its smooth functioning. The argument that Butler directs against Lacan, in other words, articulates an essential Lacanian insight.

According to Butler, Lacan's Antigone, unsupported by the symbolic order, dies as an outsider to the law. She asks (and we should again note her use of erotesis): "For Lacan, Antigone pursues a desire that can only lead to death precisely because it seeks to defy symbolic norms. But is this the right way to interpret her desire? Or has the symbolic itself produced a crisis for its own intelligibility?" (17-18). Yet to fully grasp what Lacan means by Antigone's being "eliminated from the world of the living" (*Ethics*, 280), we should note the distinction between the two deaths that Slavoj Žižek, for example, has repeatedly stressed.[3] For Lacan, the "limit zone...between life and death" (*Ethics*, 272) where Antigone finds herself, is a realm of symbolic death. In her resistance, she appeals to "unwritten laws," "a certain legality which is a consequence of the laws of the gods." "Involved here," Lacan writes, "is an invocation of something that is, in effect, of the order of law, but which is not developed in any signifying chain or in anything else" (*Ethics*, 278). Antigone's ethical call, then, responds to the beyond of symbolization, that is, the realm of the impossible real. Like all tragic heroines, she is "separated in one way or another from the structure" (*Ethics*, 271). Consequently, he argues, her refusal to follow Creon's edicts excludes her from the community, plunges her into the limbo of the living dead. By way of her ethical act, she withdraws from the symbolic order, undergoes a symbolic death. Only by understanding the two deaths, furthermore, can we appropriately map Orlando Patterson's notion of "social death," which Butler felicitously evokes (54-55), onto the Lacanian theory of tragedy and symbolic conflict.

What has always troubled Butler's reading of Lacan is her strange neglect or misunderstanding of the role of the real, a term never mentioned in *Antigone's Claim*.[4] This is particularly significant in the context of the *Ethics* seminar, where Lacan's focus shifted from the symbolic and imaginary registers to that of the real, an emphasis that became increasingly marked in his subsequent work. While one might assume that, with her description of Antigone as "the limit without which the symbolic cannot be thought" or the "unthinkable within the symbolic," Butler is pointing to the real, she goes on to identify Antigone's position as possibly embodying an "alternative symbolic or imaginary" (40). In this context, her subsequent turn to Lacan's second seminar to criticize what she considers his totalizing theory of the symbolic law is symptomatic: such a conflation of different stages in the Lacanian oeuvre allows her to overlook the role of the real in later Lacan. This elision is familiar from her earlier work. In *The Psychic Life of Power*, for example, she refers to "the unspeakable, the unsignifiable" of the symbolic order in Lacan,[5] but rather than properly naming this limit as the real, she moves on to consider the imaginary, as she does in *Antigone's Claim*. Comparing Althusserian interpellation to Lacanian subject formation, she locates the only possibility for resistance in the subject's misrecognizing the name with which the law hails her. While such misrecognition pries open a gap between the law and its actualization, allowing for inaccurate repetitions of symbolic injunctions, such resistance is unable to radically recast the terms of symbolic subjection. What Butler fails to recognize is that the only way to approach the questions of symbolic change would be to direct our attention from the question of the imaginary to that of the real.

Her idiosyncratic rendering of Lacan may be necessitated by what Butler would identify as her political concerns. She is, of course, correct in doubting the viability of a symbolic suicide as a political gesture. In Lacan, she writes, "[t]he law that mandates [Antigone's] unlivability is not one that might profitably be broken" (40). Indeed, a real act can never be undertaken for *profit*: symbolic change through the real must remain incalculable. Yet such unforeseeability of its effects necessitates it as an ethical gesture. While it seems that Butler's concept of futurity at times courts such an ethics of incalculable change, she clearly does not want to relinquish performativity's potential for strategic, "profitable" symbolic intervention, a feature that points to her theory's origin in Hegelian dialectics.

Given her thorough research of *Antigone* scholarship, what is remarkable about *Antigone's Claim* is Butler's own stubborn refusal to engage a number of recent critics who have elaborated on Lacan's ethics of the real through the Sophoclean heroine.[6] Most notably, for these writers Antigone's ethical act is more often than not radically inassimilable to Butler's theory of performativity, which in their view makes symbolic change inconceivable, dooming subjects to the imaginary repetition of symbolic edicts. Of course, the primary value of *Antigone's Claim* is not in its contribution to psychoanalytic scholarship, but in whatever political work it may inspire. What remains inexplicable in Butler's recent work, however, is her continued insistence on taking on Lacanian theory when this engagement amounts to, in effect, a non-engagement. In her many references to Lacan, she repeats the misreadings that other critics have pointed to in her earlier work, most notably concerning the category of the real. Perhaps we are to read her adamant refusal to heed the call of (what she has cast as) the Lacanian law as of the same order as that which propels Antigone's obstinacy in the face of Creon's commands. If her continued courting of and simultaneous disengagement with Lacan suggest the perseverance that also names an ethical command or responsibility, then such tragic heroism may be inspiring as a political performance. As scholarship, it is somewhat problematic.

—*Mikko Tuhkanen*

1. Jacques Lacan, *The Seminar of Jacques Lacan, Book VII: The Ethics of Psychoanalysis, 1959-1960*, ed. Jacques-Alain Miller, trans. Dennis Porter (New York: Norton, 1992), 240, 266. Subsequent references will appear parenthetically within the text. See also Caroline Rooney's discussion of Lacan and Algeria in "Clandestine Antigones," *Oxford Literary Review* 19: 1-2 (1997): esp. 52-53.

2. Erotesis is a rhetorical device whereby, instead of constructing an argument, an answer is elicited through a series of questions that in themselves imply a definite answer. For the use of erotesis in Butler's earlier work, see Tim Dean, *Beyond Sexuality* (Chicago: University of Chicago Press, 2000), 209-10.

3. Žižek makes this point throughout his work. See, for example, his "From 'Passionate Attachments' to Dis-Identification," in *Umbr(a): A Journal of the Unconscious* 1 (1998): 3-17.

4. Dean discusses Butler's failure to consider the real in her earlier work. See *Beyond Sexuality*, ch. 5.

5. Butler, *The Psychic Life of Power: Theories in Subjection* (Stanford: Stanford University Press, 1997), 94.

6. Crucial texts here include Joan Copjec, "The Tomb of Perseverance: On *Antigone*," in *Giving Ground: The Politics of Propinquity*, ed. Copjec and Michael Sorkin (London: Verso, 1999), 233-66; Charles Shepherdson, "Of Love and Beauty in Lacan's *Antigone*," *Umbr(a): A Journal of the Unconscious* 1 (1999): 63-80; and Žižek, *The Ticklish Subject: The Absent Centre of Political Ontology* (London: Verso, 1999), 263-64. Butler does briefly refer to Žižek's reading of Antigone in *Enjoy Your Symptom!: Jacques Lacan in Hollywood and out* (New York: Routledge, 1992). She writes that, as opposed to Antigone's refusal, Creon's "masculine act is apparently more affirmative for [Žižek], the act by which a new order is founded" (68). Not registering that, for Žižek, at stake in Antigone's self-destructive act is symbolic death, a withdrawal from the realm of the law, Butler wields the term "affirmative" in its commonsensical denotation, missing Žižek's point concerning the difference between Creon's *activity* and Antigone's *act*.

THE JURIDICAL UNCONSCIOUS: TRIALS AND TRAUMAS IN THE TWENTIETH CENTURY
Shoshana Felman

(Cambridge: Harvard University Press, 2002), 253 pp.

Freud had relatively little contact with the field of jurisprudence. His first and most substantial intervention was a guest lecture, the occasion for which was the recent interest taken by his audience of legal administrators at the University of Vienna in a series of word association experiments conducted by Jung. In light of then-growing suspicion of eyewitness testimony, such experimental procedures were thought to be of some legal utility in provoking criminal admission of guilt. Indeed, says Freud, in the psychoanalyst's use of certain "detective devices," the "task of the therapist...is the same as that of the examining magistrate."[1] Though he assumes here a correspondence between analyst and attorney, he is concerned that his legal audience might be overly hasty in their application of insights derived from psychoanalysis. In a gesture of feigned humility that is typical Freud, he issues the following warning: "Although my work is so far removed from the practical administration of justice, perhaps you will allow me to make one further suggestion...You might be allowed — indeed, it might be made your duty — to undertake such examinations over a number of years in every actual instance of a criminal prosecution, *without their results being allowed to influence the verdict of the*

Court" (*S.E.* 9:114). Freud's aim, Strachey tells us, as it was with his other forays into the legal field, was "to deprecate any half-baked application of psycho-analytic theories in legal proceedings" (*S.E.* 9:102). Despite Freud's best efforts, such clumsily applied psychoanalysis has made its way into both the courtroom and the legal literature. Shoshana Felman's *The Juridical Unconscious*, however, proves itself a worthy corrective.

Felman seeks to unmask the heretofore hidden link between trials and trauma, a connection that emerged, she argues, in the last half of the twentieth century: "Since the consequence of every criminal offense (as well as of its legal remedy) is literally a trauma (death, loss of property, loss of freedom, fear, shock, physical and emotional destruction), I advance the claim that trauma — individual as well as social — is the basic underlying reality of the law" (172). Felman's innovation, as we might gather from her central thesis, is not so much psychoanalytical as it is juridical. Psychoanalytic thinkers, beginning with Freud, have offered us a variety of ways of articulating the same basic truth. That trauma structures the law, this much we know. It is how we manage the traumatic gap/absence/cut/chasm/abyss that makes all the difference. Most legal scholars, much like the legal enterprise they seek to sustain, seem to prefer the avoidance method. One notable exception is Pierre Schlag, who suggestively advises "laying down the law" (a rather surprising claim to be advanced by a law professor, but this, I suppose, is part of its charm).[2] Both Schlag and Felman acknowledge that there is always something that escapes legal representation. But where Schlag finds in this failure of the law grounds for abolishing it, Felman argues that it is precisely such legal failures that serve as productive moments of transformation of and within the law.

The Juridical Unconscious opens with an examination of Walter Benjamin. Benjamin emerges as a prescient figure in Felman's analysis, which reads the Messianic promise of his Judgment Day — the day on which civilization confronts its violent history — in a secular manner, as the day history itself is put on trial, giving voice to the "expressionless" (a literary concept coined by Benjamin) of history. "In the courtroom," writes Felman, "the *expressionless* turns into *storytelling*" (14). The Nuremberg trials, then, marked something of a paradigm shift within legal history, changing as they did our idea of both the form (in the creation of new legal categories) and the function (in extending the terrain of moral deliberation) of the law. What Benjamin exposes is the contradiction inherent in the nature of the law itself: the law, and potentially every trial, is at once redemptive and oppressive. The very impossibility of redemption is what keeps the desire for justice alive. Benjamin is largely silent for the remainder of the text, as if to enact stylistically Felman's theoretical point: such silent or silenced figures speak volumes.

Armed with her reformulation of Benjamin's Judgment Day, Felman proposes a theory of "reading" trials according to the logic of repetition operative in certain legal cases — those designated "trials of the century." Following Freud's contention in *Moses and Monotheism* that the great events of history, particularly those having to do with murder, are inherently dual in nature — that the historic, traumatic force of the first event registers only in its repetition — Felman argues that the great trials of history become great trials not simply because they address (and seek to redress) traumas, but because they constitute traumas in their own right. These landmark trials are thus subject to traumatic repetition; "they too are often structured by *historical dualities*, in which a trial...unexpectedly reveals itself to be the post-traumatic legal reenactment, or the deliberate historical reopening, of a previous case or of a different, finished, previous trial" (62). Historic trials additionally "*attempt to define legally something that is not reducible to legal concepts*" (59). That the moniker, "the trial of the century," has been ascribed to a number of twentieth-century legal cases does not compromise the putative uniqueness of the trials in question so much as it underscores Felman's claim about the structural repetition of legal traumas/trials. To that end, Felman sets her sights on two of the most notorious trials of the twentieth century: those of O. J. Simpson and Adolph Eichmann.

The Simpson trial, as we know all too well, pitted two traumatic narratives against one another: the prosecutorial story of sex abuse and the defense's narrative of race abuse. The triumph of Simpson's defense team was its strategic repositioning of Simpson within the trial. The significance of his role as defendant accused of murdering his wife diminished as he was cast as the victim of black persecution, the entire history of which was brought to bear on the trial. The Simpson case accumulated legal and historical force, Felman argues, by virtue of its repetition of the relatively recent Rodney King legal debacle, as well as in light of reverberations of a more remote legal past: *Dred Scott*. If the claim that Rodney King hovered as an uncanny presence in the Simpson trial doesn't surprise us — and it doesn't — then the claim that Tolstoy does might. Felman locates striking resonances between the Simpson case and Tolstoy's *The Kruetzer Sonata*, the story of a man who, in a fit of jealousy, murders his wife and is acquitted of the crime. Following his trial, Tolstoy's protagonist narrates the story — retrospectively confesses to the crime — to a stranger on a train. In presenting the murderous husband's confession, Felman suggests, Tolstoy's novella points to what in the Simpson trial was rendered invisible: the relation between domestic violence and marriage to which we remain culturally blind. Jurors looked beyond pictures of Nicole Brown Simpson's bruised and swollen face to side with Simpson attorney Johnnie Cochran's argument that the Simpson marriage was not characterized by violence, but was simply one in which the usual level of "domestic discord" was present. "In other words," Felman writes, "the jury used the court's authority to ratify...the inherent

cultural *invisibility* of the battered face" (79). "What should have been perceived, at the conclusion of the O. J. Simpson trial is...the concrete reality of the traumatic gap — or the concreteness of the trauma. What was perceived, instead, was the abyss — the gap — between two traumas: that of race and that of gender. But race and gender differed, mainly, in this trial, in their relation to a third trauma: that of law itself" (91). In its failure to remedy the trauma — indeed, in its failure even to acknowledge the trauma that it presumed to remedy — the Simpson trial itself constitutes a trauma.

Felman carries her insight from the Simpson case — that literature opens up what is covered over by law — into her examination of the Eichmann trial. Employing Nietzschean categories of history, Felman reads the "monumental legal vision" of the Eichmann trial against the critical legal history that is Hannah Arendt's *Eichmann in Jerusalem*. Their difference turns on a matter of legal strategy. In building the State of Israel's case against Eichmann, prosecutors chose to augment documentary evidence with survivor testimony. In her effort to write a critical history, Arendt disputes the prosecutor's decision to shift the focus of the proceedings from criminal to victim. To focus on the victims, Arendt maintains, is to neglect Eichmann's crime. Felman reads a certain "jurisprudential conservatism" here, as the source of Arendt's unease — the transformation of private suffering into public pain — is, in Felman's view, precisely what the trial is about, precisely what makes it "jurisprudentially revolutionary" (122). Arendt is troubled by the failure of the Eichmann trial to establish legal precedent, but this, Felman argues, was the work of Nuremberg. The function of Eichmann's trial was to bring about instead a *"conceptual revolution in the victim*[s]," who were "for the first time gaining what as victims they precisely could not have: authority — historical authority, that is to say, *semantic authority* over themselves and over others" (126, 127).

Central to the revolutionary status Felman ascribes to the Eichmann trial was one witness in particular, one whose curious exercise of "semantic authority" became the trial's defining moment: Yehiel Dinoor, better known as K-Zetnik (a slang term meaning concentration camp inmate), who famously passed out on the witness stand. For Arendt, K-Zetnik was emblematic of all that was wrong with the prosecution's choice of witnesses. Their testimony, she felt, was largely irrelevant as it tended not to bear on Eichmann so much as on Nazi persecution more generally. (Felman points out, however, that K-Zetnik actually had contact with Eichmann at Auschwitz.) Witnesses were for the most part chosen based on their level of fame (K-Zetnik was a reasonably well-known writer) and on the heightened sensationalism of their testimony. K-Zetnik's fainting spell became, in Arendt's view, a kind of cautionary tale for the too eager witness (though Felman indicates that he had to be compelled to testify). For Felman, however, K-Zetnik's failure to deliver his testimony represents a "missed encounter between the artist and the law" (144); he shows us, in other words, that a fully legalistic understanding of the trial is impossible, that there is something in excess of the trial's legal meaning. A full appreciation of the Eichmann trial requires both a legal and a literary or artistic understanding. Beyond the requisite nod to Claude Lanzmann's *Shoah* (which, though "emblematic of art after the Holocaust and...*paradigmatic* of the work of art of our times" [152], occupies only a marginal position in Felman's present analysis), Felman argues that we derive a more comprehensive understanding of the trial from K-Zetnik, who, through the "legal failure of his testimony," created "testimonial art." "[I]t was the *inadvertent legal essence* and legal innovation and uniqueness of the Eichmann trial," she writes, "and not its testimonial accident, to voice the muteness generated by the Holocaust...The trial shows how the inherent inability to tell the story is itself an integral part of the history and of the story of the Holocaust. The function of the trial thus becomes precisely to articulate the impossibility of telling through the legal process and to convert this *narrative impossibility* into *legal meaning*" (159).

Felman successfully exposes the way in which a "juridical unconscious" necessitates the courtroom dramatization of that which cannot be articulated in legal language, of how those who have been rendered "expressionless" gain expression through the vehicle of the trial. To be sure, Felman is not alone in turning her attention to those expressionless of history, but she distinguishes her position from the often exaggerated claims made on behalf of narrative by certain feminist and critical race theorists working within the legal field, who suggest that a proliferation of personal narratives from members of subordinated groups will somehow effect a kind of moral or political improvement of the law, will somehow make the law finally recognize those to whom historically it has been blind. Felman, however, seeks not to "cure" the law of its blindness, but rather to reveal it. Narrative (the writing of history, whether literary or testimonial art) functions for Felman, that is, not to repair the fault in the law by filling the gap in legal meaning with a literary one (which is the misguided premise that governs much "law and literature" scholarship); it is rather that the literary works precisely to maintain that gap, for it is this impossibility (of telling) that articulates most forcefully the legal meaning of trauma. And it is this fidelity to the traumatic abyss — the

assumption that it is only by way of the (always missed) encounter between psychoanalysis, law, and art that one may adequately convey its meaning — that marks Felman's text as *truly interdisciplinary* legal scholarship, not the sort of "half-baked application" Freud feared.

—*Alissa Lea Jones*

1. Sigmund Freud, "Psycho-Analysis and the Establishment of the Facts in Legal Proceedings," in *The Standard Edition of the Complete Psychological Works of Sigmund Freud* (*S.E.*), ed. and trans. James Strachey et al. (London: Hogarth Press, 1953-1974), 9:108. Subsequent references will appear parenthetically within the text.

2. See Pierre Schlag, *Laying Down the Law: Mysticism, Fetishism, and the American Legal Mind* (New York: New York University Press, 1996), 166.

CONTRIBUTORS

ALAIN BADIOU is Professor of Philosophy at the University of Paris VIII-St. Denis and the Ecole Normale Supérieure. He has published a number of major philosophical works, including *Being and Event* (Seuil, 1988), *Manifesto for Philosophy* (State University of New York Press, 1999 [Seuil, 1989]), and *Ethics: An Essay on the Understanding of Evil* (Verso, 2001 [Hatier, 1998]).

ETIENNE BALIBAR is Emeritus Professor of Moral and Political Philosophy at the University of Paris X-Nanterre and Professor of Critical Theory at the University of California, Irvine. His books include *Reading Capital* (with Louis Althusser; NLB, 1970 [F. Maspéro, 1965]) and, most recently, *Politics and the Other Scene* (Verso, 2002). *We, the People of Europe? Reflections on Transnational Citizenship* is forthcoming from Princeton University Press.

MARINA DE CARNERI received her education in comparative literature and philosophy at the University of Trento in Italy, Temple University in Philadelphia, and the University of Paris VIII-St. Denis. She recently completed her dissertation, "The Subject and the Feminine," in the Department of Comparative Literature at the State University of New York at Buffalo.

STEVEN MILLER received his Ph.D. in Comparative Literature from the University of California, Irvine, in December 2002. His dissertation, "The Fulfillment of the Law: Contestation in Postwar Thought and Fiction," examines the theologico-political concept of law in Saint Paul, Kant, Arendt, Lacan, Genet, Bataille, and Beckett. He has also translated (with Jason Smith) Jean-Luc Nancy's *Hegel: The Restlessness of the Negative* (University of Minnesota Press, 2002).

KALPANA SESHADRI-CROOKS is Associate Professor of English at Boston College. She is the author of *Desiring Whiteness: A Lacanian Analysis of Race* (Routledge, 2000) and co-editor *The Pre-Occupation of Post-Colonial Studies* (Duke University Press, 2000). Her current book project, entitled *Other Difference*, addresses concepts of alterity and the limit of the human.

YANNIS STAVRAKAKIS is Humanities Research Fellow in the School of Politics at the University of Nottingham. He is the author of *Lacan and the Political* (Routledge, 1999), and co-editor of *Discourse Theory and Political Analysis* (Manchester University Press, 2000) and *Lacan & Science* (Karnac Books, 2002).

CANDACE VOGLER is Associate Professor of Philosophy and Co-Director of the Master of Arts Program in the Humanities at the University of Chicago. She is the author of *John Stuart Mill's Deliberative Landscape* (Routledge, 2001) and *Reasonably Vicious* (Harvard University Press, 2002).

SLAVOJ ŽIŽEK is Slavoj Žižek...only more so.

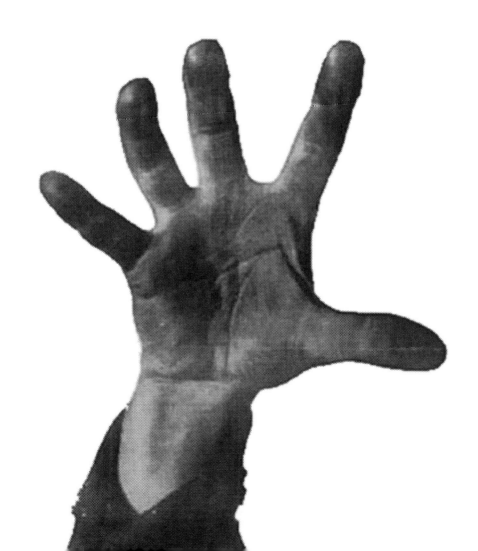

CALL FOR PAPERS
UMBR (a) 2004

ON WAR

We are at war. Since the fate of psychoanalysis has been formed by previous wars, we believe the present configuration of global conflicts to be one of these key moments in its history which simultaneously provides the object of psychoanalysis and its living context. In the next issue of **UMBR(a): A Journal of the Unconscious**, we propose to take up the relationship of world war to the very beginnings of psychoanalysis, and war's relationship to knowledge or truth, as well as the psychoanalytic concepts of war, the enemy, aggressivity, rivalry, and violence.

We also propose to analyze the new discourses on war and the enemy that have emerged in the aftermath of 9/11 and the latest war with Iraq. On a daily basis we have witnessed a complex deployment of metonymic slippages in the official U.S. discourse on the war against "our enemies," in which terms such as "weapons of mass destruction," "democracy," "liberation," "terrorist/terrorism," "war criminal," and so forth constantly shift in meaning (or perhaps, are evacuated of meaning). We hope to begin a process of unraveling this official discourse through psychoanalysis as we encounter the face of "twenty-first-century warfare" for the first time and ask the question whether it is possible to hijack the moralistic-political vocabulary of war and enemy for the purposes of radical politics.

We are currently seeking articles that engage this complex of issues. Submissions should be 1,500-6,000 words in length, must be submitted on a 3.5 diskette (MSWord) and in hard copy, and must be received no later than December 1, 2003. Please send all submissions to:

UMBR(a)
c/o Alexei Di Orio and Roland Végső
Center for the Study of Psychoanalysis and Culture
SUNY/Buffalo, North Campus
409 Clemens Hall
Buffalo, New York 14260-4610

(a)©

THE SUBJECT OF (IN)SECURITY

the journal of culture and the unconscious

A. SIMON

III:1 2003

Gabriel Riera •
"Why Insecurity?"

Tracy McNulty •
"The Limits of Fraternity"

Jeffrey Librett •
"Orientalism and Panic in
Kafka's Great Wall of China"

Anne Marie Dinesen •
"Anxiety and Modality"

Manya Steinkoler •
"Alice's Kitchen Seminar:
Homeland Security,
L'Homme Ravage and
Interior Decorating"

Dominiek Hoens •
"Badiou, Lacan and the
Subject of Uncertainty"

Gabrielle Daniels •
"Security and the Black
Female Body" and an extract
from her novel SUGAR WARS

Steven Miller •
"Psychoanalysis, Free Labor
and Capital"

Lucie Cantin •
"A Style and Ethic for the Death Drive"

Dragan Kujundzic •
"Devisions, Inscryptions and
Scenotaphs"

Sigi Jöttkandt •
"On Beckett's First Love"

©2000 Juliet Flower MacCannell for the California Psychoanalytic Circle $25/year (2 issues); institutions
$39/year email: maccannell@earthlink.net mail: (a) c/o MacCannell 2703 7th St #210 Berkeley CA 94710